I0140874

Tang Dynasty *Qian Yuan Zhong Bao* Cash Coins

Guide to Common Plain-Reverse Varieties

Tang Dynasty *Qian Yuan Zhong Bao* Cash Coins

Guide to Common Plain-Reverse Varieties

Matthew H. Dick

Published by Matthew H. Dick

Sapporo, Japan

2020

Copyright © 2020 by Matthew H. Dick

All rights reserved. This book or any portion thereof may not be reproduced or used in any manner whatsoever without the express permission of the publisher, except for the use of brief quotations in a book review or scholarly journal.

First printing: 2020

ISBN: 978-0-9910356-1-8

Email address for correspondence:
dickmatthewh@gmail.com

Dedicated to the memories of

Peng Xinwei, Chinese numismatist

and

Norman F. Gorny, scholar of Northern Song cash coins

Acknowledgements

The late Norman F. Gorny provided encouragement when I started this guide and sent me Roger Doo's book on Tang coins. Junichi Hori of Koshigaya, Saitama, Japan, taught me how to make rubbings, sent QYZB coins that he found among bulk lots of other coins, and checked the transliterations of Japanese names. Stephen Chow, a dealer whose website "xiangxiangkafeizha" is an excellent source of bulk cash coins, provided opinions or information on many relevant topics, including the minting of coins during the Tang Dynasty and the transliteration of Chinese words; he also facilitated my obtaining bulk lots of non-cleaned QYZB coins. Kyoko Takane of Sapporo kindly translated historical information from the beginning of Yoshida's book. Spiros Pavlatos of Athens, Greece, provided useful discussion as to what constitutes a variety and commented on a draft of the introductory material. My wife, Hitomi Yamamoto, was encouraging during the hundreds of hours I spent working on this guide and helped with kanji. I am grateful to all.

Preface

The two main series of bronze cash coins issued during China's Tang Dynasty (618–907 AD) bear the obverse titles Kai Yuan Tong Bao (開元通宝; KYTB) and Qian Yuan Zhong Bao (乾元重宝; QYZB). While several extensive guides exist for varieties of KYTB, less has been published about QYZB. A small book in English by Roger Wai San Doo (2003), entitled *Chronology of Kai Yuan Tung Bao*, includes 98 rubbings of QYZB. The foremost reference on QYZB is *Ken Gen Jû Hô Senfu* (Qian Yuan Zhong Bao Catalog) published in Japanese by Shôji Yoshida (2005). For value-1 coins, Yoshida numbers 123 plain-reverse varieties and 133 with reverse mark.

When I began identifying value-1-sized QYZB (smaller than ca. 26 mm in diameter) obtained in non-cleaned bulk lots, it soon became apparent that I was finding coins that I could not identify with varieties illustrated in Yoshida's catalog. I began making rubbings, and eventually arrived at the idea of a guide to the "common" QYZB occurring in these lots. The task of treating all QYZB value-1 coins was intimidating, and so I focused first on plain-reverse coins.

The title of this guide does not mean that all varieties included are equally common, or necessarily common at all, but only that I found most of them in "common," relatively inexpensive, mostly non-cleaned bulk lots. The exceptions were several separately purchased small lots of reverse-ring coins 25 mm or less in diameter, which also occasionally occur in non-cleaned lots.

Yoshida's guide is a comprehensive treatment of all QYZB, including large, officially issued value-10 and reverse-ring value-50 coins, as well as smaller, privately cast coins with reverse ring and value-1 coins with either plain reverse or reverse mark. Including many varieties known to be rare, with rubbings taken from various collections, it provides a broad classification of QYZB.

While generally following Yoshida's classification, this guide documents more extensively the fine-scale variation evident in the main groups of QYZB. It contains original rubbings and detailed descriptions for 461 coins in my collection, with no entries from other collections. It is not comprehensive, nor could it be. While it includes many varieties (or variants, depending upon how one defines varieties) not included in Yoshida's guide, the converse is also true. In fact, people attempting to identify value-1 QYZB will need both guides, and will undoubtedly still encounter coins not attributable in either. Much remains to be learned about value-1 QYZB, which will continue to make the study of these coins interesting.

Matthew H. Dick
Sapporo, Japan
July 2020

One example from each group of coins numbered in the Contents.

The page numbers are for the first page of each group rather than the particular variety shown.

Contents

As an aid in identification to group, one example from each group is shown on the facing page under the corresponding number.

Historical Context

The Tang Dynasty spanned 289 years, beginning with the fall of the Sui Dynasty in 618 AD and ending in 907 AD, when the military governor Zhu Wen deposed the last Tang emperor. It was interrupted from 690–705, when Empress Wu Zetian seized power and briefly established the Second Zhou Dynasty. The Tang Dynasty was a golden age for China, when literature, art, technological innovation, and trade flourished. The government was relatively stable during roughly the first half of the dynasty; however, the An Lushan Rebellion (also called the An Shi Rebellion, or An Shi Disturbances) from 755–763 caused widespread turmoil and destruction, and its effects weakened the power of the central government in the latter half. In all, 21 emperors reigned during the dynasty, for total periods (some of them had split reigns) ranging from 17 days to 44 years.

At its peak, the empire and protectorate states of the Tang Dynasty covered a vast region extending from the China Sea westward to what are now Afghanistan and Pakistan, and from near Korea southward to Vietnam. At the end, its human population numbered roughly 80 million. This large population meant that if coins were to be used as a medium of exchange, a lot of them were needed. Like the vast majority of coins circulating in Asia until the 20th century, Tang Dynasty coins were round with a square hole in the center; were usually made of leaded bronze; bore Chinese characters and sometimes symbols, but no images; and were produced by casting rather than striking. Collectively, Asian cast coins with a square hole in the center are referred to as "cash coins," or simply "cash."

Throughout the Tang Dynasty, the predominant coin type bore the obverse inscription 開元通宝, transliterated in the Pinyin system as Kai Yuan Tong Bao (herein abbreviated KYTB). Kai Yuan means inaugural, and Tong Bao translates literally as "circulating treasure"—in other words, currency. This Inaugural Currency was first cast in 621 to commemorate the onset of the dynasty, and its production continued for 286 years until the end. Peak production levels by official mints, though not maintained throughout the dynasty, were enormous. Peng (1994, p. 780) gave the annual output of KYTB coins during the Kaiyuan era (713–742) as 200,000 strings (each string, 1000 coins), or 200 million coins per year. The total official output during the 29-year era was 5.8 million strings, or 5.8 billion coins. In addition, possibly as many coins again were privately cast (officially sanctioned or illicit). To put these numbers into perspective, in 2019 alone, the USA (population 329 million) produced nearly 12 billion coins for circulation. While modern production levels are thus higher, minting in Tang times was done manually rather than by a mechanized process. Given the large number of KYTB produced, it is not surprising that appreciable numbers of them have survived through the past millennium to the present day.

Many of the KYTB coins were extremely well made; indeed, some of them are among the finest Asian cash coins ever produced. Their weight was initially standardized at around 1 qian (4.18 grams; Peng 1994, p. 247) and their diameter at around 25 mm; this size of coin became the ideal standard for cash coins in China, Vietnam, Korea, and Japan until the last cash coins were cast in Vietnam near the middle of the 20th century. Numismatists refer to standard-sized cash coins as having unit value, or value-1, with the higher values of larger coins expressed as multiples of value-1. In practice, even many KYTB are somewhat lighter than standard, in the range of of 3.0–3.8 grams, though some of these may not have been produced by official mints.

The KYTB issue was noteworthy for several reasons. Prior to Tang times, coin inscriptions customarily indicated the nominal weight or value of the coin; examples are 半両 (Ban Liang, or half-liang), 五銖 (Wu Zhu, or five zhu), and 大泉五十 (Da Quan Wu Shi, or large coin 50). Subsequent to the Tang Dynasty, official era names that indicated part of all of the period of an emperor's reign were generally part of the inscription. While Kai Yuan does not specify a value, it also does not refer to an era. There was a Kaiyuan era (713–742) during the reign of Emperor Xuanzong, but the inscription Kai Yuan was used long before and long after this era, and does not refer specifically to it. KYTB was the last major issue of any Asian cash coin not specifically named for a reign or era.

In addition, KYTB was the first coin to use the characters 通宝 (Tong Bao) as part of the inscription. Many of the legends on Asian cash coins issued after the Tang Dynasty contain these same two characters appended to a two-character reign or era name.

Finally, KYTB coins were among the first issues produced by sand casting (but see the following section, Production of coins) and the first major issue mass-produced in large numbers by this method. Although the Chinese had been casting complex objects in bronze for at least 2000 years prior to the Tang Dynasty, the molds used in earlier times to cast coins were made of stone, clay, or bronze. Solid molds like these were time consuming to produce and wore out relatively rapidly due to exposure to high temperature. Sand molds are easy and relatively inexpensive to produce, the sand can be reused, and the model coins used to make impressions in sand molds are not exposed to heat and do not wear out as rapidly as solid molds. Most Asian cash coins after the Tang Dynasty were produced by sand casting.

Qian Yuan Zhong Bao (乾元重宝, herein abbreviated QYZB), the subject of this guide, were the only other coins produced in large numbers during the Tang Dynasty. In 755 AD, near the end of the reign of Emperor Xuanzong, general An Lushan began a rebellion in China's northern region, declaring a new, rival Da Yan Dynasty and intending to overthrow the Tang Dynasty. At the approach of the rebels, emperor Xuanzong fled the imperial city of Chang'an and, in 756 AD, abdicated the throne to his third son, Suzong. In 758, the first year of the Qianyuan era (758–760), Suzong, strapped for cash to pay the army fighting the rebels, issued large QYZB coins. These coins had a plain reverse, weighed roughly twice as much (ca. 8 grams) as standard, value-1 KYTB coins, were larger in diameter (ca. 30 mm), and were each valued at 10 KYTB coins. The legend of these heavier coins incorporated the era title followed by Zhong Bao, meaning "heavy treasure" (see the illustration below).

Casting of the new value-10 coins led to a massive increase in illicit coining, possibly because counterfeiters could melt down two or three KYTB and re-cast them as a large QYZB worth 10 KYTB, for a profit of

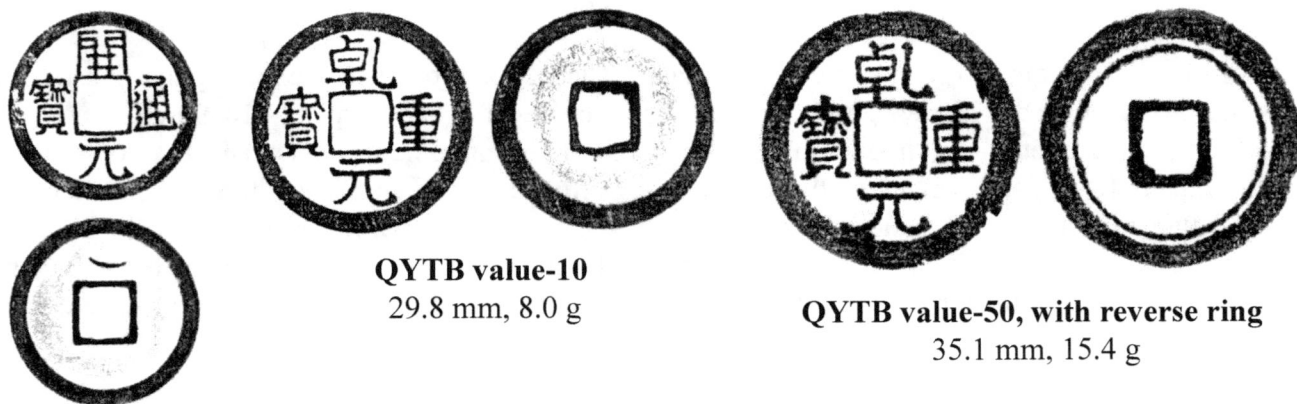

KYTB value-1
25.5 mm, 3.7 g

QYTB value-10
29.8 mm, 8.0 g

QYTB value-50, with reverse ring
35.1 mm, 15.4 g

Rubbings of a standard KYTB coin and the initial issues of large QYZB coins.

seven or eight KYTB minus the expense of casting. Despite severe repression of counterfeiters (around 800 people around the capital alone were executed for this offense), Suzong's cash-flow problems continued, and in 759 he issued larger (ca. 14–15 grams, 35 mm), value-50 QYZB coins that bore a ring just inside the reverse outer rim, a condition described as "reverse double rim" or "reverse ring." This type of coin, referred to in contemporary times as Zhong Lun (heavy wheel), proved no solution to the monetary problems, and Suzong soon devalued the value-50 coins to value-30.

At the same time, illicit minters began producing small (20–30 mm) reverse-ring coins, undoubtedly with the hope these would be valued higher than their size warranted. Doo (2003) illustrates two examples of smaller (ca. 30 mm) reverse-ring coins and lists them as "value-30," but no other sources indicate official minting of specifically value-30 coins. Instead, these were likely the beginning of the trend in downsizing of reverse-ring coins by illicit minters.

Suzong died in 762, opening the throne for his eldest son, Daizong, whose army defeated the An Shi rebels in 763. In an attempt to halt inflation, Daizong in 762 again devalued the QYZB currency: standard value-10 coins to value-2, large reverse-ring value-50 coins to value-3, small reverse-ring coins to value-2. Finally, to relieve what had become a horrible mess in currency values, he devalued all coins regardless of size to value-1.

Historical accounts do not well explain the apparently large number of QYZB value-1 coins that were produced. Hartill (2005, p. 110) gives their dates of production as 759–762. Doo (2003, p. 25) notes that Suzong cast only value-10-, value-50, and smaller value-30 coins, while all value-1 QYZB were cast by Daizong in the first year-period (Baoying, 762–763) of his reign. Doo also notes that many QYZB "of good style" were cast at local mints. According to these accounts, all QYZB value-1 coins of standard size or smaller were cast in a period of 1–3 years.

With such a short period of production, it is difficult to account for the large number of value-1 QYZB that have survived to the present. Bulk lots of these coins for sale at the time of this writing cost only 3–4 times as much as KYTB. To the extent that current market value is related to abundance, this suggests QYZB were 1/3 to 1/4 as abundant as KYTB. Even at production rates equivalent to those of KYTB, 1–3 years seems not long enough to produce this many QYZB. Looking at the problem another way, KYTB were cast for 286 years. If value-1 QYZB were cast for only 3 years at the same average rate as KYTB, their production would have been roughly 1% that of KYTB, and they should be rarer today than they are.

Peng (1994, p. 248) notes that value-1 QYZB were "probably still being minted and used after the An Shi Rebellions." Based on their relative abundance, it seems likely that these coins were produced from their appearance around 762 until the end of the Tang Dynasty in 907, a period of 145 years. One observation supporting this conclusion is as follows. In 845, near the end of the Huichang era (841–846), Emperor Wuzong allowed mints to place on the reverse side of KYTB coins a character indicating the prefecture in which the coins were cast. Twenty-three different reverse marks are known. These coins, called Huichang KYTB, are generally attributed to the year 845, although Peng (1994, p. 256) calculated on the basis of their abundance that they were probably produced for at least seven years, into the reign of Emperor Xuānzong (846–859). Cast in provincial mints, the Huichang KYTB were relatively crude. Relevant to the discussion here is that, like Huichang KYTB, similarly crude QYZB exist having provincial marks on the reverse, representing three different mints. It is reasonable to assume that these were cast at the same time as Huichang KYTB, indicating that at least some mints were still producing QYZB late in the Tang Dynasty.

Another observation indicating that QYZB were cast over a much longer period than three years is their overall variability. Doo (2005, p. 25) makes the strange statement that QYZB show "little calligraphy variation in the inscriptions." I would argue the opposite, that QYZB overall show more calligraphic variation than KYTB. Tang KYTB generally show a rather stereotyped "clerkly orthodox" script style. Nearly all, for example, have a tall, narrow YUAN with a short top bar. YUAN in QYZB varies much more, from tall to short, narrow to wide, with a long or short top bar, and with considerable differences in the shapes and lengths of the vertical strokes, or "legs." The other characters in QYZB show a similarly broad range of variation. Yoshida (2005) appears to have reached the same conclusion as I, based on variability, noting under his entry Y232 in the QYZB Towering Yuan group, "It seems that a large amount of coins were cast for a long period of time due to the considerable variation in this coin type." Admittedly, a 2008 Chinese identification guide lists 2000 varieties of KYTB, whereas Yoshida's (2005) catalog numbers only roughly 250 varieties of value-1 QYZB. However, this apparently greater diversity of KYTB might be due to a greater availability of KYTB for study, greater effort by numismatists, and/or a finer parsing of the features used to delineate varieties.

The preceding arguments for a long production of QYZB are not conclusive, and counter-arguments can be made. For example, whereas the "Kaiyuan" in KYTB was not intended as an era name, Qianyuan was an era name, and production of QYZB began in that era. The continued production of coins bearing this inscription long after the era ended would be unusual.

A few years ago, I cleaned part of a string of coins excavated in China, in which 204 value-1 coins were all cemented together in their original orientation in the string. Among these coins were 179 standard KYTB (88%), 16 Huichang KYTB (8%), 8 QYZB (4%), and one pre-Tang Wu Zhu (0.5%). Since the string contained Huichang KYTB (845–846 AD) but no coins post-dating the Tang Dynasty, it was probably strung late in the dynasty and, to the extent that it was representative, suggests that QYZB were in low proportion among cash coins circulating at the time. The apparent "commonness" of QYZB suggested by a market value today only 3–4 times as high as KYTB thus might not reflect the relative proportions of coins originally produced, but might be explained instead by dealers having culled the relatively few QYZB present in bulk lots of KYTB in order to sell the former separately at a somewhat higher price.

Though QYZB coins show considerable varietal diversity suggestive of a long production, this diversity could conceivably have been generated in a few years if a large number of mints undertook their production without much central control. After a perusal of Peng (1994), I speculate that coins were produced by at least five categories of mints in Tang times:

Imperial mints were official "coin minting inspectorates" run by the imperial government in the capital and perhaps in some other major cities.

Provincial mints were officially sanctioned and operated, but may have been largely independent of the imperial mints.

Auxiliary mints, also officially sanctioned, consisted of grants of "gift furnaces" by the emperor to members of the royal family or favored ministers, as a mark of esteem or reward for services rendered.

Permitted private mints were allowed to operate during some periods when circulating cash was in low supply and the government could not keep up with production; in such cases, the government may have simply turned a blind eye to private casting by individuals. In evidence of this, during the reign (712–756) of Emperor Xuanzong, chancellor Zhang Jiuling (673–740) worked to reduce deflation and increase the money supply by arguing in favor of private coinage.

Illicit private mints were operated against the law, and their operators were severely punished if caught.

Officially sanctioned mints, let alone private mints, were likely uncoordinated enterprises. Peng (1994, p. 251) noted for the onset of the Tang Dynasty,

"... in Wude 4 (621 AD), in addition to the capital, coin minting inspectorates had already been set up in Luozhou, Bingzhou, Yuzhou, and Yizhou. In addition, the Princes of Qin and Qi were granted three furnaces each, and Pei Ji had been given one furnace. Of these, only the coin inspectorate in the capital may be said to have been a genuine official mint. ... It is questionable whether the various prefectural and gift furnaces' coins were identical to those minted by the central government."

Official records mention that during the Tianbao era (742–756, just prior to Qianyuan era), there were 99 mints scattered across 11 prefectures (Peng 1994), a figure that may or may not include private mints and certainly not illicit mints. It is thus conceivable that several years of frantic production across many uncoordinated mints could account for the large diversity of value-1 QYZB. It is unknown which of these coins, if any, were cast by imperial mints; they may all have been produced by auxiliary, provincial, and private mints.

Production of coins

Most pre-Modern East Asian coins intended for general circulation were produced by casting rather than by striking, and most were made of leaded bronze. QYZB typically contain 60–80% copper, 10–20% tin, and 8–19% lead (Bowman et al. 2005). Many are slightly or markedly magnetic due to the inclusion of small amounts of iron as an impurity, in amounts of 0.2 to 2.1% in the coins assayed by Bowman et al. (2005).

There is controversy as to whether the Tang minters used sand molds as opposed to molds made of clay or metal. The difference is significant; molds made with casting sand do not need to be dried or fired before casting, whereas clay molds do, and sand molds disintegrate after casting whereas clay and metal molds do not. Doo (2003) concluded that the Tang minters used clay molds, based on archaeological findings of contemporaneous clay molds for coins cast in Japan, and reasoning that the Japanese would have imported the same technology as the Chinese were using at the time. He then ponders, "Why no molds for the prolific KYTB coinage have been found is thus something of a mystery." He also stated, "After Xuan Zhong (713 AD), copper molds were impressed with mother cash ... but none of these molds have ever been found." The most likely explanation why no clay or metal Tang coin molds have been found, though they have often been found at archeological sites in China from earlier eras where they were in fact used, is that the Tang minters used sand casting rather than clay or metal molds.

Although little is known of the process of casting coins in Tang times, the basic process of sand casting coins is known from later accounts (see Sung 1966, Jacobs and Vermeule 1972, Hartill 2011, Op den Velde and Hartill 2013). The first step was to carve a master model for a particular coin issue in wax (wax models are reported in Tang literature, but wood, copper, or tin could also have been used). This master was then pressed, obverse and reverse, into the two halves of clay or sand molds, and the molds used to carefully cast high-quality copies called "mother coins." The mother coins were then either used directly in mold production or, given the large numbers of model coins necessary to make impressions for mass casting, were more likely to have been used to cast numerous high-quality "seed coins" for this purpose.

Each sand mold started with two open, rectangular wooden frames (see the diagram below). One frame was set down horizontally on a flat surface, and moist casting sand was packed into it and leveled off. The seed coins were pressed flat into the sand in double columns, with a long rod or wooden strip pressed

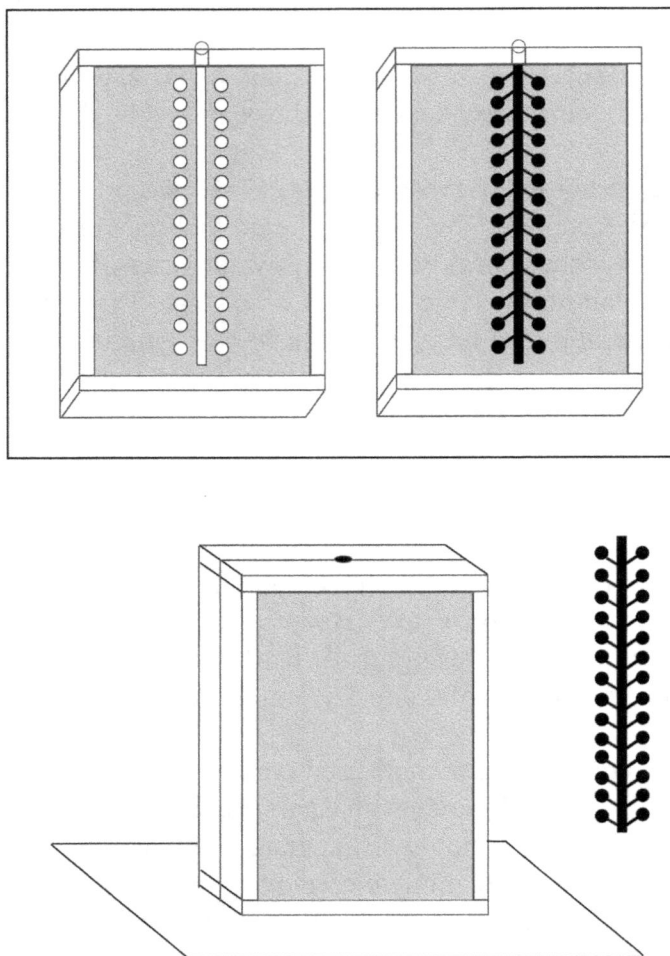

Diagram showing a sand-casting mold, with the two half-molds separated and lying flat (top), and placed together and stood on end (bottom center). The top left shows the seed coins and center rod pressed into the sand in one half-mold; these will be carefully removed before casting. At the top right, the other half-mold bears impressions from the coins and rod, with sprues having been cut between the coin impressions and the main casting channel. At the bottom center, the mold is ready for molten bronze to be poured into the hole in the top. To the right of the upright mold is the raw casting (called a "coin tree") after removal from the mold.

lengthwise between the columns to create the main casting channel (diagram, top left). The surface of this filled bottom frame (half-mold) was dusted with charcoal or some other powder to facilitate subsequent separation of the half-molds. The second frame was laid atop the first and packed with casting sand. The two half-molds, bearing obverse and reverse impressions of the seed coins, were then separated. The seed coins and rod were removed, and secondary casting channels (sprues) were gouged in one of the half-molds from the main casting channel to the coin impressions (diagram, top right). Since it would have been time consuming to lay down mother or seed coins one by one in a mold and gouge connecting casting channels each time a mold was made, I suspect that coin trees produced by casting from mother coins were in turn used intact for setting up molds during mass-casting. If this were the case, the coins on these trees cast from mother coins would be considered seed coins.

The half-molds were then reunited and securely bound together. The completed mold was stood on edge (diagram, bottom center) and molten metal poured into the main casting channel through an opening in one end. The metal flowed from the main channel into the sprues and thence into the coin impressions. After cooling, the frames were separated, exposing the casting. The sand, now somewhat stiffened by heat, was broken away from the casting and, after re-moistening, could be reused, as could the frames. The casting consisted of a "coin tree" (diagram, bottom right), with the columns of coins appearing like leaves connected by branches (the casting sprues) to a trunk (the main casting channel). The coins were clipped away from the tree and threaded in mass onto a square rod, whence their edges were filed (possibly while the rod was rotated) to remove remnants of the casting sprues. After filing, the coins were slipped off the rod, and their faces were ground and then polished by hand against a flat surface.

What is a variety?

This guide distinguishes many varieties of QYZ3 coins that differ only slightly from others in one or more features, which raises the question, what qualifies as a variety? Fundamentally, a variety should comprise all the coins descendant from a single independently designed and modeled master coin, and which all show specific features that distinguish them from other master coins and their descendants.

However, one can imagine various ways in which the boundaries of this definition might become fuzzy. Slight differences might arise, for example, if several master coins for a particular issue were carved independently based on a single drawing by a calligrapher. Or if paper rubbings made from a master coin at a central mint were sent to subsidiary mints, and those mints directed to make their own master coins as exactly as they could according to the rubbings. Or if slight casting errors among various mother coins produced from a single master coin were corrected by the minters, resulting in variation in parts of characters. Or if an illicit mint used a circulating coin made by another mint as the starting point for a model from which to create its own master coin.

Some of the differences among related coins, even slight differences, were likely intentional. From ancient times to the present, minters have used marks or other means to denote place and period of minting, a practice known as "mint control." Mint control provides a means of accounting and accountability, serving to protect governments from fraudulent practices by minters, and protect minters from accusations of fraudulent practices from governments. The most obvious forms of mint control are the inclusion of a mintmark and a written date.

For Asian cash coins having only four obverse characters and no other obverse or reverse marks, differences in calligraphy provided a means of mint control. Burger (1976, plates 7 and 8) illustrates eloquently for Qing Dynasty coins how calligraphic variation was used to distinguish among mints and among coins cast in the spring versus the autumn seasons. While information correlating possible calligraphic variants with particular mints and narrow periods has been lost in the mists of time for Tang coinage, it is certainly possible that similar means of mint control were used then.

As mentioned above, QYZB coins were produced during a time when many mints, large and small, with limited coordination among them, were casting coins. Of the 457 varieties presented in this guide, 343 (75%) are represented in my collection by only a single example. Confidence in delineating a variety increases if at least two examples are found; on the other hand, a proliferation of uncommon variants is to be expected under conditions of widespread, uncoordinated minting.

In working on this guide, I have kept in mind Masuo's (1976) classification of Japanese Ko Kan'Ei Tsûhô (古寛永通宝), in which many varieties are separated by only slight differences. Ko Kan'ei varieties are defined based on the exact shape of フ in 永 and the shapes, sizes, and positions of the dots in 永 and 通, among other minute differences. Rather than consider this variation to have arisen from an inexact casting process, Masuo appears to have proceeded under the assumption that the slight differences among coins were intentional—that they reflect design differences among the master coins used at the onset of production—and are thus meaningful.

Because so little is known about the coin casting process during the Tang Dynasty (manufacture of master coins, mother coins, and possibly seed coins), the extent to which slight calligraphic variants are meaningful is an open question. I am fully aware that I may be accused of "over-splitting," that is, of classifying so many trivial variants that the forest cannot be seen for the trees. However, I believe that only by documenting the variation in value-1 QYZB coins can the degree and significance of this variation eventually be assessed. I might add that nothing was farther from the minds of Tang minters than classificatory convenience in the 21st century.

My approach in delineating varieties has been to ask whether different variants came from different master coins, or whether two variants could be related via correction (after wear, for example) of mother coins produced from a particular master coin. Some features might theoretically be more prone to correction than others, including the length of the nose on the QIAN head, size of the dots in BAO 尔, size of the head of ZHONG, lengths of bars 1 and 2 in ZHONG; length of the top bar on YUAN, and sizes of the BAO legs. Shape changes in entire characters or in parts of characters (angles of the dots in BAO; origin and angle of the nose on the QIAN head; shapes, relative sizes, and angles of the BAO legs; shapes of QIAN 日 and ZHONG 田); changes in the relatives sizes and positions of characters; and changes in the sizes of the fields would be less prone to conversion from one form to another by correction and should be accorded more weight in classification.

In his variety guide to Northern Song coins, Gorny (2016) wrote the following in a section titled 'Variety Identification':

" ...there is absolutely no substitute for experience when classifying a coin by variety. In some series, the differences between varieties are so incredibly slight, that one might despair of ever knowing for sure if one has identified a coin correctly. ... When that happens ... keep searching for additional specimens and study them as groups, not as single coins ... The production of cash was so exact and so consistent, that one will gradually get a feel not only for what is the norm for a given cash type or variety, but also be able to tell a fake from an authentic coin, as well as a very worn one from one intentionally cast thinly."

Classification, the process by which a numismatist defines varieties and organizes them in a guide, is different from attribution (identification), the process by which the user of a guide identifies a particular coin with a defined variety. Of course, many varieties are clearly distinct from one another. However, if "the differences between varieties are so incredibly slight, that one might despair of ever knowing for sure if one has identified a coin correctly," it is possible that the classification itself is flawed, or at least ambiguous. In dealing with fine differences, the classifier must ultimately make subjective decisions, and these decisions may or may not reflect reality. In other words, neither classification nor identification is an exact science.

Taxonomists (people who classify things) are broadly divided into "lumpers" and "splitters." With regard to classifying antique Asian coins, lumpers will look for several key features, ignoring small-scale variation, in defining varieties. Splitters, on the other hand, will define additional varieties based on small-scale variation. While a guide produced by a lumper might be easier to use than one produced by a splitter, much potentially important variation will fail to be documented when, in fact, it might eventually be determined to reflect meaningful differences. There are a number of cases in this guide where several similar coins share a unique, distinguishing feature but differ in other features. Some examples are 34–38, with the right leg of YUAN recurved; 46–48, with the horizontal stroke in BAO 尔 not meeting the cap; 85–90, with a break in the side of the upper left quadrant of ZHONG 田; 108–113, with a break in the top of the upper left quadrant of ZHONG 田; 121–133, with the bars in BAO 目 tapering, acute, and often angled down to the right; 171–177, with the left side of the BAO cap short and not meeting the outer rim; 339–351, in which BAO is tilted, with the the right 貝 leg pointing toward YUAN; and 425–426, with the right side of QIAN 十 detached (Yoshida's Y113 represents another one or two varieties with this feature). The advantage in classifying variants within each set as separate numbered varieties (whether or not one agrees that they qualify as varieties) is that a rubbing is shown for each, and can be referred to by numismatists.

In practical terms, the first step in identification is to determine to which group a coin belongs, and to measure flan and field sizes. Then, focus on a particular, well-defined feature (it can be anything that stands out: shape or size of the QIAN or ZHONG head, shape of the right or left leg of YUAN, size and form of the BAO legs, rim widths, etc.) and examine your coin against coins in the guide with respect to this feature. When you find a coin having this feature, check the flan and field sizes of the candidate in the guide. This will allow you to eliminate possibilities with clearly different flan and especially field sizes. When you finally find a candidate that might match your coin, examine other features and read the description to confirm your identificaton. If one feature is unproductive, try another one. Field sizes are quite useful. When I endeavored to match coins in this guide with those in Yoshida's guide, coins that were clearly identifiable as one of Yoshida's varieties, based on idiosyncracies of the characters, usually proved to be identical in field sizes.

In using this guide, identify a coin as closely as possible but do not spend a lot of time if the identification is ambiguous; simply note what putative variety the coin is most similar to and put it aside until you can (as Gorny recommends) examine additional, similar coins together as a group. Also remember that this guide is certainly incomplete; one will eventually encounter clearly distinct varieties that are not illustrated here, and that may not have been illustrated anywhere before.

Fake QYZB

Whenever the face value of a coin markedly exceeds the value of the metal in it and the cost of producing it, there will be incentive for counterfeiters, if the potential profits outweigh the likelihood of getting caught. This has been going on for a few thousand years, wherever coins were minted. Counterfeits produced in the same period as the coins they copied are called "contemporary counterfeits" or "contemporary copies" and are as valued by collectors now as the models they were based on. In fact, many QYZB coins may fall into this category. Today, however, collectors of antique coins from all countries and eras are faced increasingly with the possibility of purchasing modern counterfeits (intended to mimic a known coin) or fakes (intended to give the impression of antiquity, whether or not they mimic a known coin). The center of production for fake antique Asian coins, as well as counterfeit modern struck coins, is China, where sophisticated workshops specialize in making fakes for the numismatic market.

A	B	C	D
27.7 mm	21.3 mm	27.0 mm	29.0 mm

E	F	G
30.8 mm	24.6 mm	23.7 mm

Fake QYZB coins encountered for sale on the Internet.

In years past, collectors bought coins from trusted dealers and actually examined the coins they wished to purchase. Nowadays, buyers on massive Internet sales outlets like eBay and Yahoo Auction Japan see only photographs of coins; sellers are more or less anonymous; and the penalty for selling fakes is minimal or nonexistent. While these outlets discourage or prohibit the sale of fakes or replicas, in practice it very difficult for them to police what is sold, for it is beyond their expertise to act as arbiters of what is genuine and what is not. On the facing page are rubbings of seven fake QYZB encountered as of December 2017 for sale on the Internet, followed by discussion for three of them as to what indicated they are fakes.

Fake A

One seller on Yahoo Auction Japan offered five of this type separately at roughly US $4.50, with two different hues of patina. This item was also for sale on eBay, where a seller in Singapore listed three separately at US $10–12 each, under the heading "Ancient China Tang Dynasty Qian Yuan Zhong Bao relic coin."

While the distinctive YUAN should allow easy identification, I could find nothing like this in Yoshida's book or other literature. If genuine, it should be uncommon or rare, and a dealer offering several at low prices was suspicious. To confirm it as a fake and examine the amount of variation among coins, I bought four for comparison. They are convincing enough that none of them appearing in a bulk lot from multiple sources might immediately be recognized as fake on the basis of superficial appearance.

Many antique Asian coins that have been buried are lightly to heavily encrusted with colorful carbonate and other minerals. Japanese numismatists call these encrusting minerals "sabi," which translates variably as rust, patina, antique appearance, or age coating. Coins that have not been buried are not heavily encrusted but have a light-green verdigris or a rich, uniform, deep-brown coloration (an aspect of sabi roughly equivalent to the term "patina" used by western numismatists). The makers of fake Asian coins cleverly apply tinted pastes to simulate the sabi resulting from burial, or use chemical treatments to simulate green or brown coloration. In the case of Fake A, the simulated sabi was slightly different among the four fake coins. What clinched them as fakes was that they were absolutely identical, down to specific defects (small nicks in the characters and rims) that in a single coin would appear to be random damage. By careful comparison, exactly the same defects could be seen in the auction photos accompanying each of the coins.

I placed one of these coins in vinegar, and the sabi came off entirely within an hour, leaving a completely bright, golden-copper-colored coin after brushing. This happens with genuine QYZB coins only rarely, when the copper content is atypically high, and never so rapidly. Genuine coins left in vinegar even for several days usually retain a pleasing, antique-brownish hue, but often also retain in places a hard, reddish encrustation that does not come off at all in vinegar or other acids. The bright coin was less convincing after losing the false sabi: the fields were uneven rather than flat, and the edges of the rims and the characters were not crisp because the faces had not been finished by abrading them on a flat surface.

Fake B

I purchased three of these coins from Yahoo Auction Japan at US $4.50 each, which is a ridiculously low price for any genuine QYZB with a reverse cloud mark. Fake B was also for sale on eBay, where the same seller in Singapore mentioned above listed two coins separately at $6 and $10, titling each as "Ancient China Tang Dynasty Qian Yuan Zhong Bao relic coin." The unusual flying-saucer-like reverse mark vaguely resembles the reverse cloud mark that appears on some genuine coins, but is too angular; Yoshida shows no mark like this. The calligraphy is also unusual; Yoshida illustrates no variety showing the combination of QIAN 乙 with a narrow base; low, broad YUAN with a raised right leg; and small, angled ZHONG head. While the coins were superficially fairly convincing due to cleverly applied false sabi and there were no obvious repetitive defects, a detailed comparison of the auction photos showed that the characters of the several coins offered were absolutely identical.

Fake C

QYZB coins with the reverse marks 東 and 國 were not cast in Tang Dynasty China but in the ancient Korean kingdom, starting in 996 AD. All varieties are rare. I purchased one coin at the remarkably low price of US $4.50 from Yahoo Auction Japan. Upon close examination, the sabi is wrong; intended to mimic the hard green malachite often appearing on ancient cash coins, it is a thin, shiny layer obviously brushed on. The characters have irregular surfaces and rounded edges. Another seller on Yahoo Auction offered an identical coin at a starting bid of US $13.50. Whereas the first seller titled it "Chinese old money" and noted in the description, "There is damage from the passing of years," the second seller noted honestly that the genuine article is very rare and that he was offering the coin "as a reference item, for the purpose of study only." The calligraphy is unlike any of the varieties of this type illustrated by Yoshida (2003) and Op den Velde and Hartill (2013).

Fakes D–G

These appeared on eBay or Yahoo Auction Japan and I examined examples of each, identifying them as fakes using the same criteria as described above. Other fakes have appeared since 2017.

Inexpensive bulk lots of Asian cash coins are unlikely to contain fakes. This is because fakes sold at only 20–80 cents apiece do not adequately compensate the effort it takes to produce them. Among bulk lots, one occasionally finds, after cleaning, uncommon or rare coins that were not previously detected because the obverse characters or reverse marks were illegible. The occurrence of a rare coin among a group of similarly dirty common coins is good circumstantial evidence that it is genuine

The general appearance of coins is not necessarily indicative of their antiquity or authenticity. Many Japanese, Korean, Chinese, and Vietnamese cash coins from 17th to 19th centuries were never buried and are very clean compared to older, excavated coins. Even some ancient and medieval coins from the Han Dynasty (206 BC – 25 AD) through the early Ming dynasty (1368–1644) have survived to the present day in remarkably good condition in strings stored in warehouses in Japan, where imported Chinese coins were circulated along with domestically produced ones. Conversely, the producers of fake coins have become so sophisticated in applying false sabi to mimic antiquity that it can be difficult to judge from photographs whether a coin is genuine.

A familiar numismatic saying is, "Buy the book before you buy the coin." For the fake QYZB illustrated here, a key indication that they were fakes was that they showed unusual calligraphy or marks that appeared in no reference books, despite the coins' relatively low prices. If one is just beginning to collect cash coins, one is well advised to stick to inexpensive bulk lots in order to become familiar with the coins and relevant literature. Furthermore, it makes sense to collect common varieties before attempting to obtain rare ones. Finally, remember that the more valuable the coin, the more attractive it will be to counterfeiters—the best of whom bought the book before they made the coin, and are so skilled that their products challenge even the experts. The book *Historical Cash Coins of Vietnam* (Barker 2004) has an excellent, well-illustrated chapter on methods used in forging Asian cash coins and how to detect forgeries. The book *Classical*

Deception (Sayles 2001) describes the extent to which fakes pervade the market for ancient and antique coins, and the consummate technical skill of the best counterfeiters.

About the rubbings

The rubbings in this guide are actual size, to facilitate comparisons with actual coins. All of them were edited with Adobe Photoshop for contrast and to remove darkened background around the coin, within the fields, and in the hole. The obverse sides of about the first 150 entries were minimally edited but checked for accuracy against the rubbed coin and slightly edited if necessary. From there until the reverse-ring coins starting at No. 410, the obverse fields were heavily edited for appearance and accuracy. The reverse-ring coins (Nos 410 to 453) were scarcely edited, except for contrast and background; the characters in this group are generally so crude that editing makes little improvement.

One reason for editing is that rubbings often do not pick up exactly what the eye sees. Rubbings "see" only what is flush with the face of the coin; parts of characters cast slightly lower than the face are often missing. For instance, only part of the ZHONG head might show in a rubbing, making it appear smaller or differently shaped than it is. Another reason is that excess metal or wear can obscure parts of characters in such a way that they are discernable in the coin but not in the rubbing. Finally, if the outer rim is raised above the level of the characters, parts of characters close to the rim will often not show accurately. As examples, ZHONG bars 1 and 2 may appear not to contact the outer rim, when in fact they do, or the legs of YUAN may appear to be raised above the outer rim, when in fact they are not. Editing can alleviate these deficiencies to some extent.

Ideally, it is best to edit rubbings as little as possible. However, many of the coins examined for this guide were poorly cast, had roughened characters due to burial and subsequent cleaning, or were to some extent worn. Sometimes, only one or two coins ideal for rubbings could be found among tens or hundreds of the same variety. When only one example of a variety was found, there was no choice but to use it for the rubbing, regardless of its condition.

In some cases, the flan size measured from a rubbing is somewhat smaller than the diameter measurement given. This can occur when the edge of the rubbed coin is rounded, rather than flat and perpendicular to the faces. In such cases, the rubbing will not pick up the true diameter as measured with calipers, and the outer rims in the rubbing will appear somewhat narrower than evident in the actual coin.

Some details of the characters in the descriptions may also differ from what is seen in the rubbings. Where discrepancies occur, the descriptions (made from the actual coins) should be considered more reliable than the rubbings.

References

Barker, R. Allan. 2004. *The Historical Cash Coins of Viet Nam. Part 1: Official and Semi-Official Coins.* COS Printers, Singapore. 386 p.

Bowman, Sheridan; Cowell, Michael; Cribb, Joe. 2005. Two thousand years of coinage in China: an analytical survey. Pp. 5–61 in *Metallurgical Analysis of Chinese Coins at the British Museum*, edited by H. Wang, M. Cowell, J. Cribb, S. Bowman. British Museum Research Publication 152, Trustees of the British Museum, London, UK. 100 p.

Burger, Werner. 1976. *Ch'ing Cash Until 1735.* Mei Ya Publications, Taiwan. 126 p.

Doo, Roger Wai San. 2003. *Chronology of Kai Yuan Tung Bao.* Shanghai Fine Arts Publisher, Shanghai. 112 p.

Gorny, Norman F. 2016. *Northern Song Dynasty Cash Variety Guide 2016.* Bookshelf Edition. Published by the Author, www.lulu.com ID 18723068, ISBN 978-1-365-05605-5. 22 + 259 p.

Hartill, David. 2005. *Cast Chinese Coins: A Historical Catalogue.* Published by the author in cooperation with Trafford Publishing, Victoria, British Columbia, Canada. 450 p.

Hartill, David. 2011. *Early Japanese Coins.* Bright Pen Publishing and Authors Online, Bedfordshire, UK. 141 p.

Jacobs, Norman; Vermeule, Cornelius C. 1972. *Japanese Coinage.* Numismatic Review, New York, USA. 151 p.

Masuo, Tomifusu. 1976. *Ko Kanei Senshi* (Ko Kanei Catalog), revised edition. Ansendo Publishing, Shimizu, Shizuoka, Japan. 148 p. (In Japanese)

Op den Velde, Wybrand; Hartill, David. 2013. *Korean Cast Coins and Charms.* Bright Pen Publishing and Authors Online, Bedfordshire, UK. 397 p.

Peng, Xinwei. 1994. *A Monetary History of China.* Volumes 1 and 2, translated by Edward H. Kaplan. East Asian Research Aids and Translations Vol. 5, Center for East Asian Studies, Western Washington University, Bellingham, Washington, USA. 930 p.

Sayles, Wayne G. *Classical Deception: Counterfeits, Forgeries and Reproductions of Ancient Coins.* 2001. Krause Publications, Iola, Wisconsin, USA. 196 p.

Scott, David A. 2002. *Copper and Bronze in Art: Corrosion, Colorants, Conservation.* Getty Publications, Los Angeles, California, USA. 515 p.

Sung, Ying-Hsing. 1966. *Chinese Technology in the Seventeenth Century.* Translated and annotated by E-Tu Zen Sun and Shiou-Chuan Sun. Dover, Mineola, New York, USA. 372 p.

Yoshida, Shôji. 2005. *Ken Gen Jû Hô Senfu* [Qian Yuan Zhong Bao Catalog]. Aokura, Kyoto, Japan. 120 p. (In Japanese, with English translation of preface).

Terminology

On the following two pages are illustrations dealing with terminology. By necessity, Western numismatists transliterate the reign or era titles written on antique Chinese coins into Romanized Chinese. The first illustration shows terminology applied to the main parts of QIAN, YUAN, ZHONG, and BAO, labeled with the Pinyin Chinese transliterations. In the facing illustration, details of the characters are labeled with the English terms used in the descriptions.

In a sort of linguistic schizophrenia, the group names listed in the Table of Contents are the Japanese names translated from Yoshida (2005), because Yoshida's is the only comprehensive classification of QYZB of which I am aware. Along with the translated names in the Contents are the original names in Japanese. In the text, each group name is followed by the original name in Japanese and the Romanized Japanese transliteration. Incidentally, virtually all of the kanji, or characters, in the Japanese group names are common to both Chinese and Japanese. A Chinese reader seeing Yoshida's group names in Japanese will be able to pronounce them in Chinese and have some sense of their meaning. To illustrate the differences in pronunciation, the transliteration for 乾元重寳 is "qian yuan zhong bao" in Mandarin Chinese and "ken gen jû hô" in Japanese; parallel transliterations for 乙 are "yi" and "otsu"; for 田, "tian" and "ta." In the descriptions in the text, I avoided having to choose between the alternative readings of 日, 十, 乙, 田, 貝, 目, 王, and 尔 simply by using the kanji rather than transliterations.

In their catalogs and guides, Japanese numismatists give both numbers and descriptive names to their varieties. This has the advantage that, whereas different guides in Japanese may number a variety differently, the name will remain the same, leading to easy cross-reference. Western numismatists typically use only numbers, and the numbers from different guides must be cross-referenced. In this guide, I only number the varieties, but I include Yoshida's numbers (prefixed by 'Y' and suffixed with 'U' or 'L' to refer to his upper or lower rubbings) for varieties that I was able to cross-reference between the two guides.

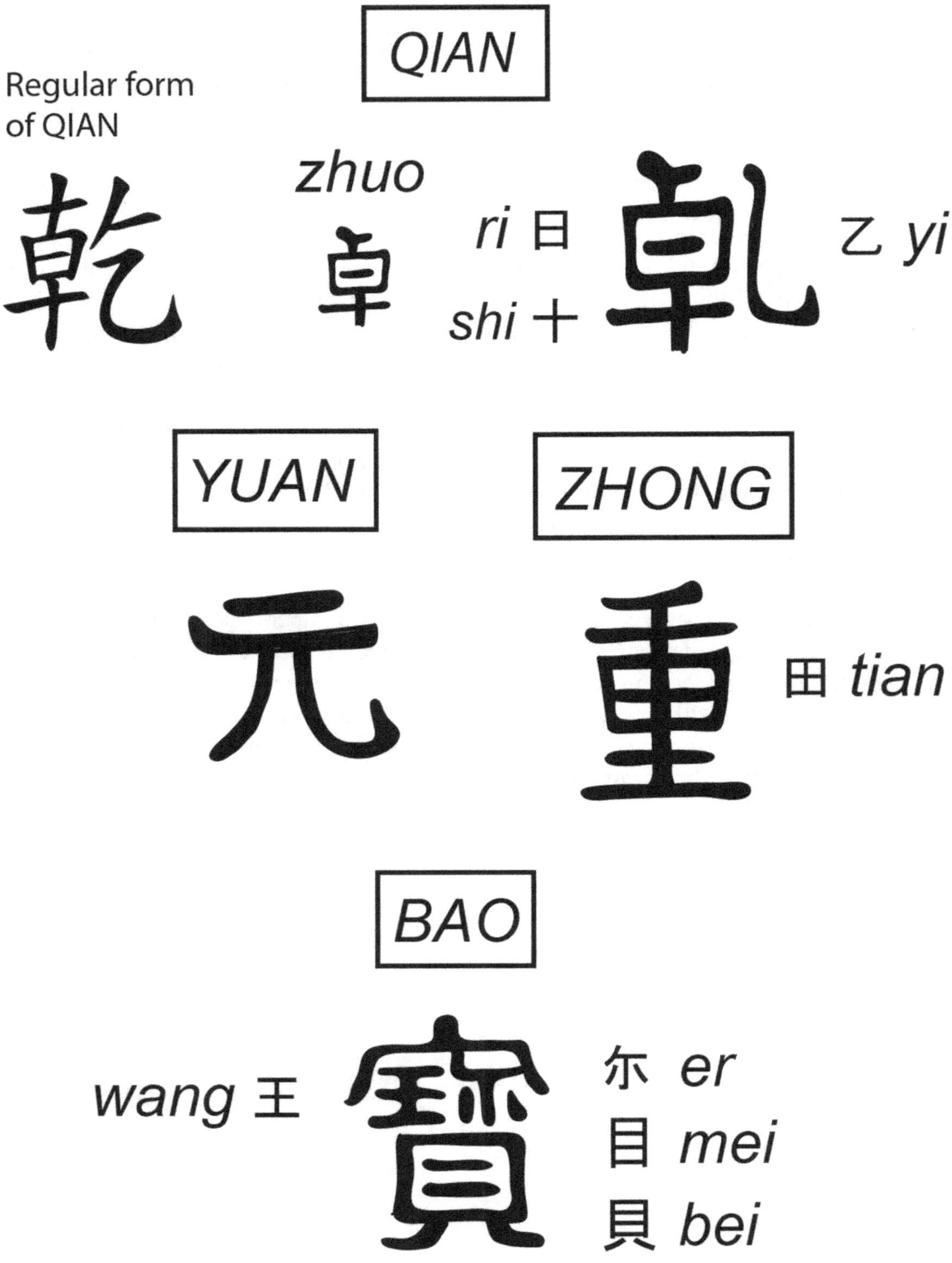

QIAN

Regular form
of QIAN

乾

zhuo 卓

ri 日
shi 十

軋

乙 yi

YUAN

元

ZHONG

重

田 tian

BAO

wang 王

寶

尔 er
目 mei
貝 bei

The four characters on QYZB coins, with the main parts labeled in Pinyin Chinese transliteration.

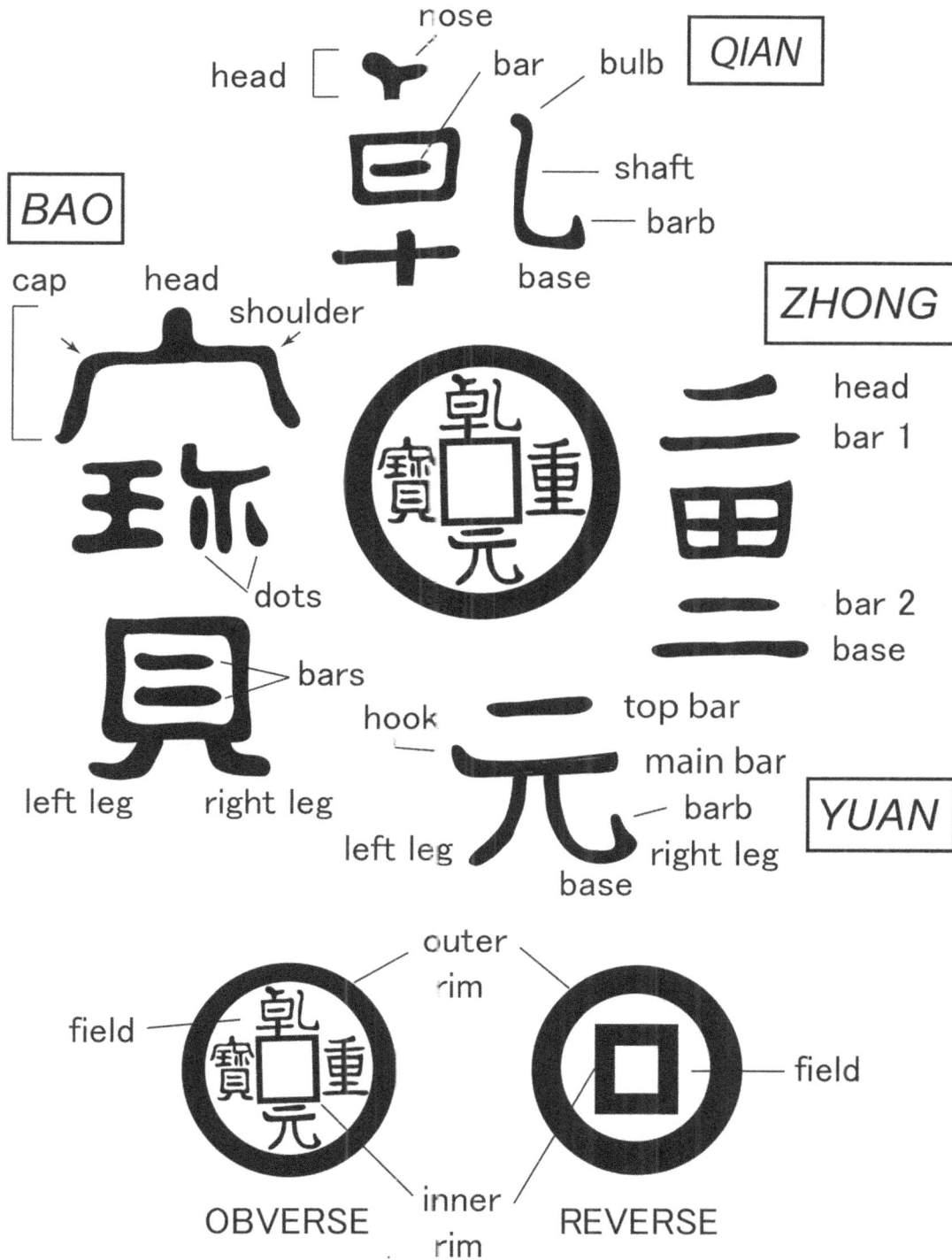

Descriptive terminology for identifying features of QYZB coins.

Identifying features

Field sizes

I have used field sizes (diameters) as an important tool for delineating varieties. Two coins with clearly different field sizes cannot have been cast from the same model, especially if the obverse and reverse sides do not vary in the same direction—for example, if one coin has a smaller obverse field but a larger reverse field than the other. Similar-seeming coins with different field sizes often show subtle differences in other features upon close examination. Field sizes are a more reliable identifying feature than outer-rim widths or coin diameters, as the latter two can vary with the degree of edge filing during the finishing stages of minting. Of course, field sizes alone cannot be used for identification, because varieties that are clearly different can have exactly the same field sizes.

One way that field sizes might vary slightly within a variety is if a circulating coin were used as a seed coin during minting, for example by an illicit minter who did not want to make his own model. Due to the shrinkage of bronze upon cooling, the coin produced would be 1–2% smaller than the seed coin. However, this amount is essentially undetectable with the method described below for comparing field sizes. Another way field sizes can vary is due to wear (see the next section). I tried to use the least-worn examples of coins for rubbings, but sometimes a worn coin was the only example of a variety in possession and had to be used.

Field sizes can easily be measured from coins and compared with actual-size rubbings or with other coins, or measured from rubbings and compared against coins. To measure field sizes, simply lay a strip of paper against the obverse side of a coin or rubbing and mark the widths of the field and inner rim, then turn the coin over and make the corresponding marks for the reverse, as shown in the diagram below. The strips can be any size; I use strips about 3 cm wide, cut from a blank sheet of typing paper across the width. Obverse and reverse measurements from 12 coins can be put along both edges of both sides of a strip this size.

Fields are not always symmetrical—the size measured along one axis can differ somewhat from that measured along another—but this variation can be marked on the strip as well. In this guide, I have tended to use the phrase "field size similar" where a field size in one variety fell within the range of variation due to asymmetry in another variety, and "field size the same" or "field size as in..." where symmetrical fields were the same size.

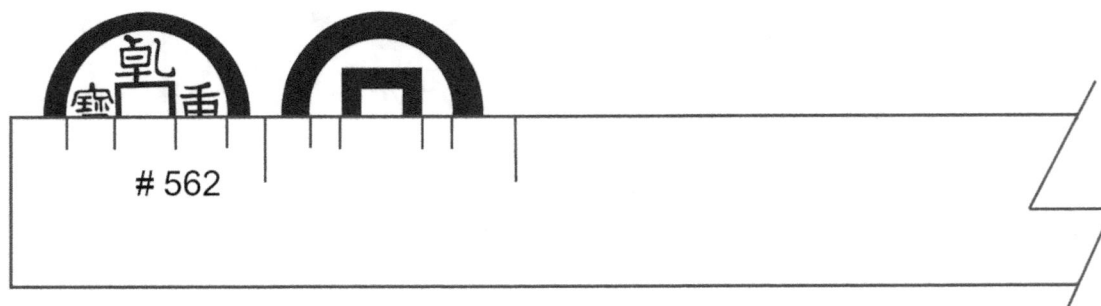

Method for comparing field sizes among rubbings and coins.

The descriptions in the text compare field sizes from one variety to another. Comparing each variety to the variety preceding it led to "creeping field sizes," whereby similarities and differences among many varieties were not immediately apparent, without tracing back through a long string of comparisons. To avoid this problem, I arbitrarily chose reference varieties within groups, and compared the field sizes in other varieties to those.

Effects of wear

Wear can affect various features of a coin—field sizes, rim widths, and the characters themselves. The illustration below shows four rubbings from the same coin. The minimally worn coin illustrated by the rubbing at the far left was subjected to three equal intervals of artificial wear by abrading it against a piece of fine sandpaper laid flat, with a rubbing made initially and again after each round of abrasion. Compared to the coin at the left, the artificially quite worn coin at the right appears to have larger characters; the head of QIAN is larger and touches the outer rim; the head of ZHONG is larger and thicker; the bars in BAO 貝 appear to be nearly complete rather than short and centered; the outer rims are wider; and the fields are slightly smaller. The outside diameter in the far-right rubbing is a little larger than in the far-left rubbing, but this can be explained by the edge of the starting coin being rounded rather than perfectly perpendicular to the face of the coin. Wear is a factor affecting both the delineation and identification of varieties, and is a potential source of error in this guide.

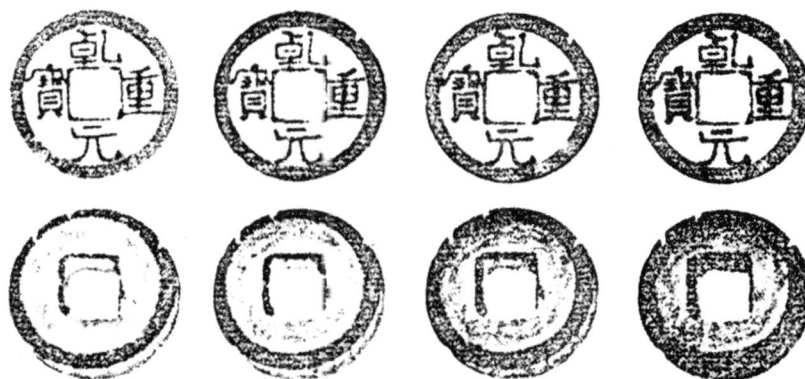

From left to right, effects of wear on a single coin.

Other features

Character sizes can also vary between varieties, but unless the size differences are pronounced, they are difficult to judge accurately between two coins. Bright coins often falsely appear to have larger characters than dark coins of the same variety, and the effect wear has just been described. The positions of characters relative to the inner and outer rims (for example, BAO close to the inner rim, or evenly spaced between the inner and outer rims) are more useful features than character size.

Varieties will generally differ from one another in particular combinations of features, rather than in a single feature. On the following pages are illustrations showing some of the variation in the characters or their parts. It will be productive for the reader to examine these illustrations in some detail before using this guide, to become aware of the features useful in identification.

Variation in parts of the characters in QYZB coins, part I

QIAN head. Straight and either vertical **(b)** or tilted **(f)**, but usually slightly or markedly curved **(a, c, d, e, g)**. Nose at the top **(a)**, middle **(b, d, e, g)**, near the base **(c)**, or at the base **(f)**. Nose horizontal **(a, b, d, e)** or clearly angled upward **(c, f, g)**.

Bar in QIAN 日. Incomplete: short and centered **(a)**, long and centered **(b)**, centered in reduced, rounded space **(c)**, shifted right **(e)**, or shifted left **(f)**. Complete: evident in rubbing **(d)**, or weak and below level of coin face **(g)**, not showing in rubbing.

Shape of QIAN 日. Rectangular or nearly so **(a, b)** or nearly square **(c)**; squared on one side and tapering on other **(d)**; tapering more on one side than other **(e)**; tapering on both sides **(f, g)**.

QIAN 十. Symmetrical and tall **(a)** or short **(b)**. Asymmetrical, with horizontal stroke above middle **(c, d)** or shorter on one side **(d, f, g)**. Reaching inner rim **(a–d, f)** or not **(e, g)**.

QIAN 乙. Reaching outer rim **(1c, 1d, 1g, 2a, 2b, 2d)** or not **(1a, 1b, 1e, 1f, 2c, 2e–g)**. Shaft with bulb rounded **(1b, 1d, 1f, 1g, 2c, 2e)**, hooked **(1e)**, acute **(1a, 2g)**, minimal or lacking **(2a, 2d, 2f)**. Base rounded **(1a, 1g, 2c, 2g)** or angular **(1b–f, 2a, 2b, 2d–f)**. Angular base right-angled or nearly so **(1b, 1c, 1d, 2a, 2d–f)**, or angled down **(1e, 1f, 2g)**. Base narrow **(2b, 2c)**, moderately wide **(1a, 1b, 1d, 1e, 1g, 2a)**, wide **(1c, 1f, 2d, 2e)** or very wide **(2f, 2g)**. Base extending beyond edge of inner rim **(1c)**. Barb strong **(1c, 1f)**, weak **(1g, 2c, 2f, 2g)**, or moderate (the rest).

YUAN. Tall **(1e, 1f, 2d, 3e, 3f)**, short **(2a, 2c, 3c, 3g)**, or intermediate (the rest). Legs not reaching **(1a)**, incised from **(2f)**, or just touching outer rim **(1b, 3g)**. Left leg **(1d, 1f, 1g)** or right leg **(1c, 3a)** raised from outer rim. Left leg **(2b, 2f, 3c)** or right leg **(1e)** recurved. Left leg short, shallowly curved **(2e, 3d, 3g)** or long, more deeply curved or angled **(1c, 2a, 2c, 3a)**. Right leg deeply **(e.g. 1a, 1g, 2a)** or shallowly **(e.g. 1c, 2e, 3d, 3g)** curved, with base curved (e.g., 1a) or flat **(1g)**. Right leg with back-angled barb **(1b, 3a, 3b, 3f)**, vertical barb **(e.g. 1d, 2a, 2d)**, or barb scarcely evident **(3e, 3g)**. Barb weak **(e.g. 1c)** or strong **(e.g. 1a, 1d, 3b, 3f)**. Top bar short **(1c, 2c, 2e, 2g, 3b, 3e, 3g)** or longer (the rest). Main bar with sharp left hook **(2c, 2d, 2g, 3c)**, almost no hook **(1b)**, or intermediate (the rest). Main bar truncate **(3b)**.

ZHONG head. Triangular **(1a–c)**, curved **(1d–g, 2a)**, irregular **(2b)**, straight **(2c, 2d)**, or degenerate **(2e-g)**. Large **(e.g. 1a–d)** or small **(e.g. 1e–g, 2a, 2d)**. Reaching inner rim **(1c)** or not (the rest).

Zhong 田. Rectangular **(1a–c, 2d)**, shorter on one side than the other **(1d, 1f)**, more strongly tapering on one side than the other **(1e, 1f, 2b)**, tapering about the same on both sides **(1g, 2a, 2c, 2e, 2f)**. Centered on vertical stroke **(e.g. 1b, 1f)** or not **(1c, 1e)**. Middle horizontal stroke off-center **(2e)** or incomplete on one or both sides **(2c, 2d, 2f)**.

	a	b	c	d	e	f	g
QIAN head							
QIAN 日 bar							
日 shape							
QIAN 十							
QIAN 乙 1							
2							
YUAN 1							
2							
3							
ZHONG head 1							
2							
ZHONG 田 1							
2							

Variation in parts of the characters in QYZB coins, part 2

ZHONG base. Complete, reaching inner and outer rims **(a)** or incomplete, not reaching outer rim **(b, c, d)**, inner rim **(e)**, or either rim **(f, g)**. Angled or curved up or down **(d)** or more or less horizontal (the rest). Zhong bars 1 and 2 can also be complete or incomplete, reaching only inner or only outer rim, or neither.

BAO head. Wide and tall **(a, b)** or short **(c)**, small **(g)**, or narrow **(d–f)**.

BAO cap. Sides more or less symmetrical **(1a–d, 1g)** or asymmetrical, with different angle on one side than other **(1e, 2b–f)**. Sides short **(1c)**, long **(1b, 2e)**, or intermediate (the rest). Left side not reaching **(1a, 1b, 2a, 2b)** or reaching (the rest) outer rim. Cap tilted down to left **(1e)** or right **(1g)**.

BAO 王. Most common condition is with long horizontal strokes **(a, b)**. Sometimes thick, ladder like **(c)**, or vertically or laterally compressed **(d–f)**. Often compressed **(e)** or irregular **(g)** in small coins (< 22 mm).

BAO 尔. Dots small **(1a, 1c)**, larger **(1b, 1d, 2c)**, or linear **(1e–g, 2a, 2b)**. Dots symmetrical **(1b, 1d, 2a 2c)** or of different size **(1a, 2b)** or set at different angles **(1a, 1e, 1g, 2b)**. Left dot angled **(2a)** versus vertical **(2b)** is important feature in some groups. Horizontal stroke sometimes disconnected from cap on right side **(1d)**, top **(not shown)**, or entirely **(2e)**. Conspicuously m-shaped **(2e, 2f)** in some groups. Center vertical stroke sometimes detached **(2c)**, reduced **(2f)**, or missing **(1f)**. Dots fused to horizontal stroke along with vertical stroke **(2d, 2g)**, or right dot and vertical stroke making inverted 'V' **(1g)**. In some cases, the difference between similar varieties can be clear-cut size differences in 王 or 尔 or both.

BAO 目 bars. [Also referring to rows 1–3 under "BAO legs" following]. Complete **(a, 1e)**, long and centered in normal **(b, 2e, 3c)** or rounded **(e)** space, short and centered **(c, 1b, 2a, 2b, 2d, 2f, 3b, 3d, 3f)**, shifted left **(d, 1f)**, shifted right **(2g, 3e)** connected left **(f, 1c)**, tapering and slanting down to right **(g)**, irregular **(1a, 1d, 1g, 2c)**. Whether bars are connected (versus shifted) left or right, or complete versus long and centered, is sometimes ambiguous in worn coins. In less-worn coins, the bars will show a slight gap or suture from the side(s) if they are shifted rather than connected, or incomplete rather than complete.

BAO 貝 legs. Large **(1b, 1d, 1f, 2e, 2g)**, small **(1c, 2d, 2f, 3a)**, or intermediate **(1a, 2a, 2b, etc.)**. Symmetrical or nearly so **(1a–d, 2f, 3c)** or asymmetrical (larger, longer, or lower on one side than other) **(1e–g, 2a–d, 3a, 3b, 3d–f)**. Right-angled **(1a, 1b, 1f, 2a–c)**, straight **(3c–e)**, blunt **(2g, 3a)** or curved **(1c, 1d, 1g, 2d–f, 3b, 3f)**. Directed horizontally **(e.g. 1a, 1b, 2a, 2b)**, curved upward **(1c, 2e, 2f)**, or directed downward **(1e, 2g, 3e, 3f)**. Reaching only outer rim **(1f, 3c–e)**, only inner rim (2c), both rims (1g, 2e), or neither rim (1a, 1b, etc.). Whether or not the legs reach one or both rims is to some extent dependent on degree of wear; a leg close to a rim in an unworn coin may reach the rim in a worn coin.

BAO. BAO can be vertically compact **(a–c)** or relaxed **(d–g)**.

Breaks. Breaks in characters in certain positions help define some varieties: top right of BAO 貝 **(a, b)**; side **(c)** or top **(d)** of upper left quadrant of ZHONG 田; top right of 田 **(f)**; in middle horizontal stroke of 田 **(e, f)**; and in upper right side of BAO cap **(g)**. There are others. For varieties represented by a single coin, it is ambiguous whether a break is due to a casting error, or characteristic of the variety.

	a	b	c	d	e	f	g
ZHONG base							
BAO head							
BAO cap 1							
2							
BAO 王							
BAO 尔 1							
2							
BAO 目 bars							
BAO 貝 legs 1							
2							
3							
BAO							
Breaks							

QUICK ID

The QUICK ID on the opposite page shows the 20 QYZB varieties most commonly encountered among the approximately 2600 coins I examined, in order of decreasing abundance by percentage of the total. Together, the first 10 varieties comprised 60% of all coins examined, and the 20 varieties shown in the QUICK ID comprised 70%. The cut-off at 70% was arbitrary; two other varieties were as common as 198, with percentages gradually tapering off from there among many other varieties. The QUICK ID is a good place to start for identification—there is a 60% chance that a random QYZB coin you encounter will be one of the first 10 varieties, and a 70% chance it will be among the 20 shown here. If you think you have one of these, go to the page indicated to confirm the ID. For most of the groups represented in the QUICK ID, there are additional varieties besides these common ones, but chance favors your coin being common. The key to symbols below indicates the groups to which the most common varieties belong, along with the starting page for each group. Seven of the most common varieties belonged to the Wide Characters, Prancing Yuan group, which collectively comprised roughly 20% of all coins examined. The Towering Yuan group was next most common, comprising roughly 18%.

☾	**WIDE CHARACTERS** — p. 40
✳	**WIDE CHARACTERS, PRANCING YUAN** — p. 58
†	**STRONG YUAN** — p. 68
§	**TOWERING YUAN** — p. 74
279	**WIDE HOLE** — p. 76
‡	**WIDE HOLE, THIN CHARACTERS** — p. 78
Δ	**WIDE HOLE, SWOLLEN CHARACTERS** — p. 78
◊	**LOW HEAD TONG, LOW YUAN STYLE** — p. 96

Explanation of guide entries

Number of coins of this variety found among approximately 2600 coins examined.

Rubbing at actual size.

← **Variety number.**

← **Diameter** or range of diameters.

← **Yoshida's (2005) number** for this variety, preceded by 'Y', with the suffix 'U' or 'L' indicating the upper or lower entry in Yoshida's guide when the entry here is more similar to one than to the other.

← **My rubbing number.**

404	
24.1–24.4 mm	
5	Y337U

875

QUICK ID

265 - p. 74	211 - p. 62	279 - p. 76	299 - p. 78	219 - p. 64	303 - p. 79
11.7%	8.3%	7.9%	7.2%	6.7%	5.8%
§	*		Δ	*	Δ
243 - p. 68	271 - p. 74	295 - p. 78	244 - p. 68		393 - p. 96
5.4%	3.6%	1.8%	1.7%		1.6%
†	§	‡	†	← 60%	◊
272 - p. 74	188 - p. 60	298 - p. 78	268 - p. 74	180 - p. 58	193 - p. 60
1.5%	1.1%	1.0%	1.0%	0.9%	0.8%
§	*	‡	§	*	*
224 - p. 64	85 - p. 42	198 - p. 60			
0.8%	0.6%	0.5%			
*	☾	*	← 70%		

Value-1 coins (小平錢, *shô hei sen*)

PROPER CHARACTERS (正字, *sei ji*)

The QIAN head is back-curved, with the nose usually angled up; the bar in 日 is incomplete, centered in a rectangular field. ZHONG is vertically compact; 田 is narrow and closer to the inner than the outer rim. BAO 貝 has short or long, incomplete bars that are centered or not; the legs are typically angular, tapering, and horizontally directed. Some or all characters are separate from the outer rim. This group is quite similar to the Large Characters group (group after next), but the latter differs in QIAN 日 typically having a long or complete bar, often set in a space with rounded inside corners, with the top of 日 often convex, and in BAO 貝 having the bars complete or nearly so, often in a reduced space; the BAO legs are usually curved rather than angular, and are not always horizontally directed. Yoshida numbers four plain-reverse varieties in the Proper Characters group, and no varieties with reverse mark.

1 - All characters well separate from outer rim. BAO with bottom bar of 貝 shifted left; legs angular, left leg blunt, right leg smaller and acute, neither reaching adjacent rim.

2 - Fields as in 1. QIAN with head just touching outer rim. YUAN left leg long, thin distally, just touching outer rim. BAO with head of cap narrow, slightly off-center; 貝 narrower than in 1, bars centered; legs small, thin, angular, acute, nearly symmetrical, neither leg reaching adjacent rim.

3 - Fields as in 1. QIAN head reaching outer rim; nose horizontal. YUAN with both right and left legs reaching outer rim. BAO legs long, tapering; left leg longer, reaching outer rim, right leg not reaching inner rim.

4 - Fields as in 1; outer rims narrower. Characters similar to 1, but QIAN with head taller, close to but incised from outer rim; vertical stroke in 十 tilted to right. YUAN with longer left leg. BAO legs nearly symmetrical, both acute.

5 - Very similar to 4; obv. field same size, rev. field slightly smaller. Characters quite similar, but in 5 all characters appear larger, more robust. Right end of ZHONG bar 1 touching upper right corner of 田. Compared to 4, BAO with 王 wider, dots in 尔 heavier, 貝 legs larger, rounded, symmetrical.

6 - Fields similar to 5, characters larger. QIAN, ZHONG heads larger. BAO 目 with upper bar complete, lower bar connected left; BAO legs asymmetrical, left larger than right.

7 - Flan, fields, characters somewhat larger than in 1. Characters similar; all separate from outer rim. QIAN head thicker; 乙 with sharp angle between shaft and base. BAO 貝 with both bars in center; right leg longer than left; in rubbed coin, center horizontal stroke of 王 incised from vertical stroke on each side, appearing as two dots.

8 - Obv. and rev. fields smaller than in any previous vars. ZHONG, BAO separate from outer rim. QIAN head unusual in shape; 乙 shaft with thick bulb. YUAN top bar tapering to point on left; left leg slightly raised from outer rim; right leg touching rim at turn of barb. BAO 貝 with upper bar shifted right; BAO legs small, angular, right leg slightly larger, neither touching adjacent rim.

9 - Characters thin. Obv. field as in 8, rev. field larger, as in 1. QIAN head small, nose horizontal. YUAN left leg long, reaching outer rim; right leg shallowly curved, base narrow, just touching outer rim at turn of barb. ZHONG head thin. BAO 貝 with bars long, centered; legs small, thin, angular, asymmetrical, left leg

1	2	3	4	5	6
25.0–25.4 mm	25.5 mm	25.2–25.5 mm	25.2 mm	25.5 mm	25.2 mm
2 Y128U	1	1	1	1	1
37-r2	923	1050	249	738	904

7	8	9	10	11	12
25.8 x 26.4 mm	23.8 mm	24.2 mm	23.9–24.4 mm	24.2–24.7 mm	24.3 mm
1	1	1	2	2	1
735	742	716	497	752	712

not reaching outer rim, right leg longer, reaching inner rim.

10 - Fields slightly smaller than in 1. QIAN, ZHONG, BAO not touching outer rim. QIAN head strongly back-curved. YUAN left leg reaching outer rim, right leg incised from outer rim in one coin, merged with rim in other. BAO 王 large, with larger interval between lower two horizontal strokes than between upper two; 尔 with horizontal stroke angled down to right; BAO 貝 legs thick, horizontal, blunt, left larger than right; neither touching adjacent rim.

11 - Fields slightly larger than in 10. All characters but ZHONG touching outer rim. YUAN with long left leg just touching outer rim; right leg meeting outer rim at turn of barb; barb long, thin. BAO legs angular, asymmetrical, left thick, right thin, each nearly reaching adjacent rim.

12 - Fields as in 11. ZHONG, BAO not touching outer rim. QIAN head with nose near base, angled up; barb on YUAN right leg angled strongly backward. BAO 王 tall, with horizontal strokes sloping; BAO legs small, left shorter and thicker than right, neither leg reaching adjacent rim.

13 - Very similar to 12; field sizes same. QIAN, ZHONG, BAO separate from outer rim. QIAN head smaller. BAO 王 not tall, with horizontal strokes perpendicular; dots in 尔 small. BAO left leg angled downward.

14 - Fields small, similar to 8; rev. outer rim wide. ZHONG, BAO separate from outer rim. QIAN head tall, nose horizontal. YUAN left leg reaching outer rim; right leg raised, incised from rim. BAO legs angular, asymmetrical; left leg thicker, not reaching outer rim; right leg reaching inner rim.

15 - Obv. field similar to 14, rev. larger. Only ZHONG clearly free from outer rim. QIAN head thick, nose short, near middle, angled up. YUAN left leg long, reaching outer rim; right leg touching rim at turn of barb. BAO legs asymmetrical; left leg larger, angular, meeting outer rim; right leg smaller, curved, meeting inner rim. Outer rims narrower in rubbed coin than in other, probably due to variation in edge filing.

16 - Fields as in 15. QIAN head in rubbed coin poorly cast. YUAN main bar sloping down to left; with long left leg meeting outer rim; right leg with strong barb, angled strongly backward. ZHONG with narrow 田; base short, distant from outer rim. BAO legs moderately long, nearly symmetrical, left leg not reaching outer rim, right leg just touching inner rim.

17 - Obv. field as in 15; rev. field smaller. Rubbed coin worn, some details missing. QIAN, BAO not reaching outer rim. QIAN head short, with nose slightly angled up. YUAN left leg with angular bend; right leg deeply curved, with long barb. ZHONG closely appressed to inner rim, head reaching inner rim, bars 1 and 2 long, reaching outer rim. BAO legs asymmetrical, left thicker than right.

18 - Obv. and rev. fields smallest in this group; ZHONG, BAO small, not touching outer rim. QIAN head large; right side 十 horizontal stroke detached. YUAN left leg long, reaching outer rim; right leg incised from rim. BAO with 貝 bars short, thin, centered; legs small, symmetrical, acute; neither leg touching adjacent rim. Field sizes as in Yoshida's Y130 and characters quite similar, but 18 has larger QIAN and ZHONG heads and detached right side of 十 .

PROPER CHARACTERS, WIDE YUAN
(正字濶元, *sei ji katsu gen*)

Similar to the Proper Characters group above. QIAN is short; YUAN appears off balance, being wide and spread out, with the right leg shallowly curved. Yoshida numbers two vars, both plain reverse.

19 - QIAN, ZHONG well separate from outer rim. BAO bars long, centered. QIAN 乙 with conspicuous bulb and strong barb. YUAN with main bar slightly tilted down to left; left leg long, straight toward end, meeting outer rim; right leg raised from rim. BAO cap with large, bulbous head; 貝 legs small, acute, nearly symmetrical, both turned up.

20 - Fields as in 19. Characters very similar, but QIAN with smaller head and smaller barb on 乙. Barb on YUAN right leg small. BAO cap with small head; dots in 尔 thin, linear; 貝 legs asymmetrical, left larger than right.

21 - Narrower obv. outer rim than in preceding two vars; rev. field asymmetrical. QIAN head thick; 乙 base right-angled, with long base and small barb. Right leg YUAN reaching outer rim at turn of barb. ZHONG head damaged, incomplete in rubbed coin. BAO cap with small head; 貝 legs similar to 19. Rubbed coin with hole damaged, transversely enlarged.

13	14	15	16	17	18
24.7 mm	24.6 mm	23.8–24.5 mm	24.1–24.3 mm	23.7 mm	24.2 mm
1	1	2 Y127U	1	1	1 cf. Y130
713	52	718	452	54	740

19	20	21			
25.5 mm	25.4 mm	24.5 mm			
1 Y131U	1 Y132L	1			
358-r2	358-r1	1046			

LARGE CHARACTERS (大字, *tai ji*)

This group resembles the Proper Characters group above in having ZHONG vertically compact, with 田 relatively narrow and conspicuously closer to the inner than the outer rim. In the Large Characters group, QIAN 日 typically has a long, nearly complete bar, often set in a space with rounded inside corners; the top of 日 is sometimes slightly convex. BAO 貝 usually has long or complete bars; the legs are typically curved rather than angular, and not always horizontally directed. The characters in this group are not necessarily large; the group name refers instead to similarity in the form of the characters to larger (ca. 30 mm), value-10 coins, which are not treated in this guide. Yoshida lists 32 varieties in this group, of which six have a plain reverse. While the Large Characters group is collectively fairly common, I found no varieties that were particularly abundant. This group needs much more study.

22 - Large flan, narrow outer rims. Characters reaching close to but not touching outer rim (right leg YUAN probably incised from rim in unworn coins). BAO legs blunt, not angular, nearly symmetrical, neither touching adjacent rim; right leg reaching below level of inner rim. Rev. inner rim moderately wide. Rubbed coin worn.

23 - Fields as in 22; characters very similar, but QIAN head shorter and thinner, with longer nose; space inside 日 reduced, with rounded inside corners. ZHONG head uniformly thick, blunt. Rev. inner rim narrow. Excess metal obscuring ZHONG and BAO in rubbed coin.

24 - Fields slightly larger than in 22; all characters touching outer rim. QIAN head large; nose below middle, angled up. YUAN left leg long, merging with outer rim; right leg with heavy, triangular barb, touching outer rim along base of barb. BAO with thick bars centered in reduced space; legs thick, slightly angled down, asymmetrical, right leg thicker, not touching inner rim, left touching outer rim. Rubbed coin worn.

25 - Fields slightly smaller than in 22. ZHONG, BAO free from outer rim. QIAN tall; head with nose near middle, horizontal. YUAN left leg shallowly curved, reaching outer rim; right leg with small, triangular barb. BAO with dots in 尔 vertical; bars in 貝 short, centered in oval space; legs acute, left thicker than right, neither leg touching adjacent rim.

26 - Fields as in 22. Hole large, obv. inner and outer rims narrow. QIAN head with nose below middle. YUAN left leg shallowly curved, merging with outer rim, right leg reaching outer rim at turn of barb. ZHONG head thin, tapering. BAO 尔 dots distinct, linear, angled; bars in 貝 long, complete or nearly so in reduced space; legs thin, nearly symmetrical, neither touching adjacent rim.

27 - Rev. field as in 22, obv. field slightly smaller. Hole large, all rims thin. All characters except QIAN meeting outer rim. Top of QIAN 日 convex, center bar incomplete, shifted right; 乙 with sharp barb. BAO with 貝 bars nearly complete; legs thin, nearly symmetrical, left meeting outer rim, right not meeting inner rim.

28 - Rev. field smaller than in 27, rev. inner rim wider. Characters similar to 27, but QIAN head shorter, back-curved; ZHONG head thicker; left dot in BAO 尔 linear, vertical.

29 - Obv. field as in 22, rev. field slightly smaller; characters smaller. All characters reaching outer rim. QIAN head with short, horizontal nose in middle; 乙 with hooked bulb, small barb. YUAN main bar with almost no hook. ZHONG head thin. BAO with dots in 尔 small; 王 with horizontal strokes short, in low relief, vertical stroke thick; 貝 legs tapering, neither quite reaching adjacent rim.

30 - Fields markedly smaller than in 22. QIAN head incised from outer rim, nose below middle; bar in 日 long, centered. Right leg YUAN touching rim at turn of barb. BAO 貝 bars long, incomplete, connecting

22	23	24	25	26	27
25.6–26.0 mm	26.0 mm	26.2 mm	26.1 mm	25.2–25.5 mm	25.2 mm
2 cf. Y152	1	1	1	2	1
1049	905	744	253	929	17-B

28	29	30	31	32	33
24.6 mm	26.2 mm	25.4 mm	25.4 mm	25.8 mm	25.2 mm
1	1	1	1	1	1
931	930	241	501	753	17

left, upper bar tapering; legs asymmetrical, left thick and blunt, right thin and acute, neither quite touching adjacent rim. Left dot in BAO 尔 linear, vertical; right dot teardrop shaped, angled out.

31 - Similar to 30, but rev. field somewhat larger. BAO 貝 with bars complete in reduced field; legs asymmetrical, left leg tapering and reaching outer rim, right leg longer, blunt, not reaching inner rim.

32 - Fields similar to 22, but characters smaller. QIAN, YUAN, ZHONG reaching outer rim. QIAN with tall head, nose short, below middle, angled up; bar in 日 nearly complete. YUAN with only slight hook on main bar; right leg broadly meeting outer rim. BAO with dots in 尔 small, left dot vertical; bars in 貝 irregular, shifted left; legs small, splayed, horizontal, right leg lower, neither leg meeting adjacent rim.

33 - Fields similar to 22. Characters not touching outer rim. QIAN with 日 bar short, centered; head short, with long nose angled up. YUAN main bar with conspicuous hook, nearly reaching BAO. ZHONG head long, thin. BAO with 貝 bars long, incomplete; legs symmetrical, splayed, blunt, neither leg touching adjacent rim; legs lower than bottom of inner rim.

Next five vars have right leg of YUAN recurved, markedly so in 34–36, less conspicuously in 37 and 38. Also see vars 52, 53, 57.

34 - Fields as in 30, smaller than in 22. All characters touching outer rim. QIAN head with long nose angled up; bar in 日 nearly complete; 十 tilted to left. YUAN right leg recurved; raised from outer rim. BAO with 貝 bars nearly complete; legs asymmetrical, left thicker, reaching outer rim, right not reaching inner rim.

35 - Fields as in 30. QIAN head with short, needle-like nose; bar in 日 complete, with break in middle; 乙 bulb hooked. YUAN right leg strongly recurved, broadly meeting outer rim. ZHONG 田 wide. BAO 貝 with bars shifted left in reduced space; legs asymmetrical, left thicker and touching outer rim; right thin, reaching corner of inner rim.

36 - Obv. field slightly smaller, rev. field slightly larger than in 30. All characters tilted to right. QIAN tall; 乙 bulb conspicuous, hooked; 日 bar long, connected right. YUAN right leg strongly recurved, incised from outer rim. Right side of ZHONG 田 broken in rubbed coin. BAO 王 small, 尔 irregular; 貝 legs thin, left longer and touching outer rim, right distant from inner rim. Rev. inner rim narrow.

37 - Obv. field similar to 30; rev. field larger. QIAN with 日 bar short, centered; head with nose at base, angled up. YUAN right leg mildly recurved, raised from rim; barb small, blunt. BAO with 貝 bars thin, incompletely cast; legs nearly symmetrical, horizontal, neither leg touching adjacent rim.

38 - Obv. field slightly smaller, rev. similar to 30. Characters small. QIAN with 日 bar complete or nearly so; QIAN head thin, with nose below middle, angled up. YUAN with slightly recurved right leg, incised from outer rim; barb small. ZHONG head small, thin; ZHONG bar 2 short on left side. BAO with dots in 尔 linear, nearly vertical; space in 貝 reduced, with rounded inner corners, bars nearly complete; legs nearly symmetrical, each nearly meeting adjacent rim.

39 - Fields slightly smaller than in 30. QIAN 乙 with wide base, short barb. YUAN with both legs incised from outer rim. ZHONG with 田 nearly rectangular, without tapering sides. BAO 貝 with both legs thick; left leg angled slightly down, reaching outer rim; right horizontal, not reaching inner rim. Rubbed coin poorly cast and worn, but key features visible.

40 - Fields slightly larger than in 30. QIAN 日 vertically compressed, nearly rectangular; incomplete bar connected right. YUAN right leg deeply curved, touching outer rim at turn of heavy, blunt barb. ZHONG head thin. BAO 貝 with incomplete bars in reduced space; legs small, left larger than right, neither reaching adjacent rim.

41 - Fields larger than in 30. QIAN head unusual; large, with top curved far back against outer rim (error due to excess metal near head?); nose long, connected below middle, slightly angled upward. YUAN right leg deeply curved. BAO legs thick, asymmetrical, left larger than right, neither touching adjacent rim.

42 - Fields similar to 30. QIAN head incised from outer rim (meeting rim in worn coin), nose below middle, horizontal; bar in 日 long, nearly complete. ZHONG 田 touching inner rim. BAO 貝 with complete bars in reduced, circular space; legs large, rounded, close to but incised from adjacent rims; right leg angled downward, reaching slightly lower than inner rim.

34	35	36	37	38	39
25.2 mm	24.5 mm	25.1 mm	25.6 mm	24.1–24.5 mm	25.0 mm
1	1	1	1	2	1
375	455	571	743	495	1047

40	41	42	43	44	45
25.8 mm	25.3 mm	24.6–25.1 mm	25.3 mm	24.7 mm	24.6 mm
1	1	2	1	1	1
138	932	754	1032	727	494

43 - Obv. field as in 30, rev. field markedly larger. ZHONG, BAO not reaching outer rim. QIAN with tall head, long nose near middle, slightly angled up; 日 with long, centered bar and rounded inner corners; bottom of 十 incised from inner rim. ZHONG head thin; bar 1 not reaching inner rim. BAO legs small, nearly symmetrical, distant from adjacent rims; 貝 with break at top upper left; bars centered in normal space.

44 - Field sizes as in 43; differs in having narrower outer rims and rev. inner rim; QIAN head smaller, with nose more sharply angled up; YUAN left leg longer, merging with outer rim; BAO 貝 with bars shifted left in reduced space; legs similar.

45 - Fields similar to 30. QIAN head with thin nose below middle, horizontal; bar in 日 incomplete, connected right. YUAN right leg with wide, flat base. BAO 貝 with incomplete bars shifted left in reduced, circular space; legs asymmetrical, left thicker and meeting outer rim, right not meeting inner rim.

Vars 46–48 have in common a small ZHONG head; horizontal stroke of BAO 尔 not reaching right side of cap; bars in BAO 貝 complete in reduced, circular space; BAO legs large; hook on main bar YUAN scarcely evident.

46 - Obv. field similar to 30, rev. field larger. QIAN head with nose below middle, slightly angled up; bar in 日 complete, in oval space. ZHONG 田 not close to inner rim, appearing to be rectangular but partly obscured in rubbed coin. BAO not touching outer rim; 貝 legs asymmetrical, right longer, neither touching adjacent rim.

47 - Like 46, but QIAN head larger, with nose near middle, horizontal. YUAN right leg more deeply curved, meeting rim at low angle. ZHONG 田 squared on left, tapering on right. BAO touching outer rim; 貝 legs asymmetrical, left larger and touching outer rim, right not touching inner rim.

48 - Like 46, but QIAN head smaller, with thin nose near middle, horizontal; 日 bar incomplete, incised at ends, in nearly normal space; bulb of 乙 circular, distinct. ZHONG 田 tapering on both sides. BAO not touching outer rim; 貝 legs thick, nearly symmetrical, neither leg touching adjacent rim.

49 - Fields larger than in 30, smaller than in 22. Characters thin, small relative to flan size. ZHONG, BAO not meeting outer rim. QIAN, YUAN tall. YUAN with short top bar; right leg with tiny, sharp barb. Coin with slightly rolled rim (i.e., raised edge around circumference of each face).

50 - Fields similar to 30. QIAN head small, not touching outer rim; nose tiny, near middle, horizontal, detached. YUAN with short top bar; left leg long, meeting outer rim, right leg incised from outer rim. BAO 尔 with small dots; 貝 legs asymmetrical, left leg reaching outer rim; right leg quite thin, not reaching inner rim.

51 - Obv. field as in 30, rev. somewhat larger. QIAN head tall; 日 bar complete. YUAN main bar lacking hook. ZHONG head thin, horizontal. Top of BAO cap narrow; 貝 with bars complete, in reduced space; legs small, left leg slightly thicker and touching outer rim, right free from inner rim.

52 - Obv. field slightly smaller than in 30, rev. slightly larger. QIAN with 日 bar long, connected right; head with nose below center, angled slightly up. Left leg YUAN meeting outer rim; right leg slightly recurved, raised from rim. ZHONG head straight; left side of ZHONG bar 2 detached. BAO 貝 with bars incomplete, lower bar shifted left; space not reduced. BAO legs asymmetrical; left thick and blunt, right thin and acute; neither touching adjacent rim.

53 - Rev. field as in 30, obv. slightly smaller. QIAN with bar in 日 nearly complete, shifted right; head small, with thin nose below middle. YUAN right leg incised from outer rim. BAO with side of cap on left closer to adjacent rim than that on right; cap head acute; 貝 bars nearly complete in normal space; legs thin, acute, angled down, neither leg reaching adjacent rim.

54 - Fields similar to 53. Characters very similar, but QIAN head thick. Bar in QIAN 日 long, centered; BAO with 尔 right dot and vertical stroke forming inverted V; 貝 bars incomplete in reduced space. Rubbed coin has left side 貝 broken.

55 - QIAN head large, with long nose below middle, angled up; 日 with bar nearly complete in reduced space. YUAN right leg broadly meeting outer rim, base narrow, barb blunt. BAO 貝 with incomplete bars in reduced, circular space. BAO legs thick, blunt, nearly symmetrical, left leg meeting outer rim, right leg incised from inner rim.

56 - Very similar to 55, but fields slightly smaller; obv. outer rim wider. Horizontal stroke in QIAN 十

46	47	48	49	50	51
25.0 mm	24.3 mm	25.4 mm	26.0 mm	25.3–25.7 mm	24.5 mm
1	1	1	1	2	1

730   717   1031   500   564   737

52	53	54	55	56	57
24.8 mm	25.2 mm	24.6–24.8 mm	24.2 mm	24.8 mm	24.6 mm
1	1	2	1	1	1

722   683   1040   1037   607   266

58
24.3 mm
1

261-A

short, thin on right side; 乙 base extending past edge of inner rim. YUAN right leg more deeply curved. BAO legs asymmetrical, left thicker, reaching outer rim; right angled down, not reaching inner rim.

57 - Fields similar to 56. QIAN head with nose slightly angled up; bar in 日 complete; 乙 with hooked bulb. YUAN right leg incised from outer rim, slightly recurved. BAO with 貝 bars complete in reduced space. BAO legs asymmetrical, left thin and acute, right thicker and blunt, neither touching adjacent rim.

58 - Obv. side crudely cast. Obv. field as in 57, rev. slightly larger. QIAN head unusually short, irregular; bar in 日 incomplete, shifted right in normal space; left and right parts of QIAN touching one another; 乙 with narrow base, sharp, back-angled barb. YUAN left leg long, meeting outer rim at low angle; right leg meeting outer rim at turn of barb; barb long. ZHONG head large. BAO with blunt head on cap; 貝 legs rounded, nearly symmetrical, each just touching adjacent rim; left leg turning slightly upward.

59 - Fields smaller than in 30, especially reverse. Obv. outer rim narrow to moderately narrow. Rev. outer and inner rims moderately wide. QIAN with thick, erect head, small nose below middle; bar in 日 centered in reduced space; 乙 bulb enlarged, circular. ZHONG head large. YUAN left leg not deeply curved, meeting outer rim; right leg broadly incised from rim (merged in worn coins). BAO with head of cap tall, tapering; 貝 with long, incomplete bars connected left; legs thin, angled slightly down, left meeting outer rim, right longer, not meeting inner rim.

60 - Fields similar to 59. QIAN head thin, curved, with long nose in middle, slightly angled up; 日 narrow, scarcely tapering, bar complete; 乙 with wide base, barb long and thin. YUAN right leg with broad base, barb blunt. ZHONG short, with thin head; 田 narrow. BAO with cap not touching outer rim; head tiny; center vertical stroke in 尔 tapering; bars in 貝 complete in reduced, circular space; legs asymmetrical, left angled down, just touching outer rim; right more horizontal, incised from inner rim. This coin might have a reverse crescent or bar below the hole, but it is so faint as to be questionable.

61 - Rev. field as in 30, obv. field smaller. QIAN head tall, long nose in middle; 日 strongly tapering on right, bar long, incomplete. YUAN with right leg well appressed to outer rim, barb blunt. ZHONG short; head long, thin; 田 scarcely tapering. BAO cap with small head; 貝 bars incomplete in normal space; legs asymmetrical, left thick and reaching outer rim, right thin, not reaching inner rim. Coin with slightly rolled rim (i.e., raised edge around circumference of each face).

62 - Fields smaller than in 30. QIAN head small, with short nose near base, angled up. YUAN right leg broadly meeting outer rim. BAO narrow; 王 narrow, ladderlike, with thin horizontal strokes; bars in 貝 complete, in reduced space; legs asymmetrical, right longer than left, each close to but incised from adjacent rim.

63 - Fields slightly smaller than in 62. Characters small, tilted to left; hole large; obv. inner rim unusually thin. QIAN head tall, angled but not curved, with short nose near base; 日 bar complete. Left leg YUAN shallowly curved, right leg meeting outer rim at turn of barb. BAO small, 貝 bars nearly complete; legs thin, similar to those in 62, each touching adjacent rim.

64 - Fields similar to 63. Characters similar, but not tilted; obv. outer rim narrower. QIAN head slightly curved; short, horizontal nose near middle; bar in 日 complete. YUAN left leg with very shallow curve. BAO legs as in 63 but thicker. Coin with slightly rolled rim (i.e., raised edge around circumference of each face).

65 - Small flan, fields; obv. outer rim narrow. Characters tilted slightly to right. QIAN with short 十. YUAN short, right leg deeply curved. ZHONG with thick head; 田 unusually wide for this group, with unusually thick sides. BAO 貝 legs asymmetrical, right thicker than left.

66 - Rev. field as in 65, obv. slightly larger; obv. outer rim narrow. All characters tilted strongly to left. Hole large. QIAN head erect, with short nose below middle; 日 bar complete, in oval space. YUAN right leg broadly touching outer rim. ZHONG head similar to but thinner than that in 65. BAO short; cap with acute head; bars in 貝 complete.

67 - Fields similar to 66, obv. outer rim thin. Characters large, thick; QIAN tilted to right; obv. inner rim complete, moderately wide compared to 66. QIAN head erect, short nose near base; 乙 with thick, blunt barb; 日 with incomplete bar in oval space. YUAN left leg deeply curved; right leg broadly meeting rim, with sharp, triangular barb. ZHONG head thick, irregular. BAO 貝 with complete bars in reduced space; legs robust, asymmetrical, right longer than left, each meeting adjacent rim.

59	60	61	62	63	64
22.7–23.7 mm	23.9 mm	23.8 mm	23.2 mm	23.7 mm	23.2 mm
7	1	1	1	1	1
239	724	652	621	682	1064

65	66	67	68	69	
21.8 mm	22.1 mm	22.3 mm	23.7 mm	22.8 mm	
1	1	1	1	1	
156	281	1058	721	928	

68 - Obv. field as in 63; rev. larger. Characters tilted slightly to right. QIAN head short, curved, with long nose in middle, angled down; 日 bar centered. YUAN left leg long; right leg touching outer rim toward turn of barb; barb acute, tilted toward ZHONG. ZHONG head small; bar 2 short. BAO cap asymmetrical, head wide, triangular; 三 small, tilted to right, 尔 irregular; bars in 貝 short, centered; legs asymmetrical, right longer, neither touching adjacent rim, both curving up slightly.

69 - Obv. field smaller than in 63, rev. field similar. Hole small, inner rim distinct. QIAN head short, curved; 日 scarcely tapering, 日 bar centered; 乙 with wide base extending well past inner rim, barb long. YUAN left leg short, scarcely curved; right leg broadly contacting outer rim. ZHONG head small, irregular; ZHONG base raised above bottom of inner rim. BAO 尔 dots linear, left dot strongly angled, right dot nearly vertical; 貝 with incomplete bars; legs thin, curved, splayed, each just touching adjacent rim. Rev. inner rim moderately wide.

70 - Obv. field as in 69, rev. field smaller. Characters tilted slightly to left. Obv. outer rim narrow; obv. inner rim thin. QIAN head erect; 日 with complete bar, in oval space. YUAN right leg evenly curved. ZHONG head long, thin, reaching inner rim. BAO 貝 with complete bars; legs asymmetrical, right longer, each touching adjacent rim.

71 - Fields markedly smaller than in 63; outer rims moderately wide. QIAN tilted slightly to right; 日 bar incomplete, centered in oval space. YUAN right leg deeply curved, touching outer rim at turn of barb in unworn coin. ZHONG head thick, nearly reaching inner rim. BAO 尔 with vertical stroke and right dot forming inverted V; 貝 legs asymmetrical, left leg angled down, just touching outer rim; right leg longer, thicker, more horizontal, reaching corner of inner rim.

LARGE CHARACTERS EVENLY SPACED IN FIELD
(大字狭穿, *tai ji kyô sen*)

Similar to the Large Characters group, but ZHONG 田 and BAO 目 are more or less evenly spaced between the inner and outer rims, QIAN and YUAN are both free from the outer rim, and ZHONG is more relaxed than is typical for the Large Characters group. Yoshida numbers four varieties, two of which have a plain reverse.

72 - Except for ZHONG bar 1, characters not touching outer rim. QIAN 日 and BAO 貝 with short, centered bars. ZHONG separated from inner rim; with break in upper left quadrant of 田 near vertical stroke. BAO 尔 appears to have three dots (vertical stroke detached).

WEAK FORM (容弱, *yô jaku*)

The characters are thin and crudely cast. The head of QIAN is tiny. The base of ZHONG is straight, raised above the bottom of the inner rim. Yoshida numbers six vars, of which only one has a plain reverse.

73 - QIAN small, with tiny head; 日 with short, centered bar; 乙 with strong barb. YUAN raised above outer rim; left leg short; right leg recurved, with strong barb. ZHONG small; raised somewhat above level of bottom of inner rim; base straight. BAO 貝 with short, centered bars; legs small, right larger than left, neither touching adjacent rim.

70	**71**		**72**		**73**
21.8 mm	22.4–22.5 mm		25.1 mm		23.3 mm
1	2		1	Y183U	1	Y200
723	510		858		1063

WIDE CHARACTERS (濶字, *katsu ji*)

YUAN is wider than tall. ZHONG is vertically compact, with 田 wide, close to the inner rim and nearly reaching the outer rim. QIAN 乙 is usually L-shaped, with the base at roughly a right angle to the shaft. Yoshida lists four plain-reverse varieties (Y133–Y136) and two with reverse mark. The coins in this section are arranged roughly in order from YUAN having the left leg relatively short and shallowly curved to having it long and deeply curved. All features contribute to defining varieties, including differences in field sizes; the size and shape of the QIAN head; the shapes of both legs of YUAN; the size and shape of the head of ZHONG; the bars in QIAN 日 and BAO 貝; the size, shape, and orientation of the BAO legs; the dots in BAO 尓; the widths of the outer rims; and gaps or breaks in some places in some characters. This is a large, difficult group, with much fine-scale variation.

Vars 74 to 84 very similar, with small differences in sizes and shapes of QIAN head, 日 and 貝, and dots in 尓. 74 and 75 have break in upper right corner of BAO 貝.

74 - Bar in QIAN 日 long, incomplete, centered; QIAN head with nose near middle, angled up. ZHONG head small; 田 with left side squared, right side longer than left, tapering, with acute upper-right corner. BAO with dots in 尓 elongate, both angled out; 貝 with break in upper right corner; bars long, incomplete, centered; legs small, curved, nearly symmetrical, directed laterally, neither touching adjacent rim. Two examples shown.

75 - Smaller flan, narrower outer rims, slightly smaller obv. field than in 74. Break in BAO 貝, as in 74. Left side ZHONG 田 tapering.

76 - Field sizes similar to 74. Characters similar, but BAO without break in upper right corner of 貝. QIAN head taller, straighter. YUAN taller, with longer left leg merging with outer rim. BAO legs small, angular, acute, asymmetrical, left larger than right, neither reaching adjacent rim.

77 - Obv. field slightly smaller than in 74. QIAN head with nose high, touching outer rim; upper right corner of 日 acute. YUAN left leg raised from outer rim. BAO legs nearly symmetrical, tapering, reaching inner and outer rims; left leg angled up.

78 - Coin asymmetrical. Field sizes on short axis as in 74. Very similar to 77. QIAN head with nose above middle. YUAN left leg raised from outer rim. ZHONG not touching inner rim. BAO extending higher than top of inner rim.

79 - Similar to 74, but upper right corner of BAO 貝 without break. QIAN head larger, nose horizontal. YUAN right leg more broadly meeting outer rim. ZHONG with larger head; upper right corner of 田 not particularly acute. BAO 貝 with bars shifted left; legs angular, asymmetrical, left markedly larger than right, tilted slightly up, touching outer rim; right tiny, not touching inner rim.

80 - Fields similar to 74. QIAN head short, not strongly curved, nose long, above middle. YUAN right leg angular, base straight, touching outer rim only at turn of barb. ZHONG 田 wide, touching inner rim and nearly reaching outer rim, scarcely tapering; ZHONG head larger. Left dot in BAO 尓 vertical; 貝 trapezoidal, shorter on left than on right; legs angular, horizontal, asymmetrical, left larger and touching outer rim, right nearly touching inner rim.

81 - Similar to 80, but BAO with larger head on cap; both dots in 尓 angled out, right dot exaggerated, teardrop shaped.

74 #1	74 #2	75	76	77	78
24.0–24.7 mm		22.8 mm	24.7 mm	24.3 mm	24.2 x 24.7 mm
10		1	1	1	1
11-D	11A	562	1052	460	1033

79	80	81	82	83	84
24.3–24.5 mm	24.7 mm	24.2–24.3 mm	24.2 mm	24.2 mm	23.8 mm
3	1	2	1	1	1
733	729	1085	688	755	748

82 - Fields as in 74. QIAN head curved, with short nose in middle strongly angled up; 日 without acute upper right corner. YUAN left leg raised from outer rim; right leg with rounded base. ZHONG 田 strongly tapering on both sides; reaching inner and outer rims. BAO 貝 legs asymmetrical, left leg angular, acute, right leg larger and rounded, each leg just touching adjacent rim.

83 - Very similar to 82. QIAN 十 with thick vertical stroke, but not tilted to left as in next var. YUAN right leg with flat base, touching outer rim only at turn of barb. BAO cap wider; 貝 legs markedly larger, longer than in 82; asymmetrical, right leg thick, left thinner, tapering, tilted slightly down; each connecting with adjacent rim.

84 - Fields similar to 74. QIAN head curved, with nose near middle, slightly angled up; 十 tilted to left. YUAN right leg with broader base than in 83. BAO legs thin, angular, not tapering, nearly symmetrical, each reaching adjacent rim; left leg slightly angled up.

The following six vars have break in vertical stroke at upper left corner of ZHONG 田.

85 - Obv. field smaller than in 74; rev. field similar. QIAN head with nose slightly above middle, horizontal; 日 bar incomplete, centered. Left leg YUAN short, not quite reaching or incised from rim. ZHONG head small, longer than in 74; top right corner of 田 not conspicuously acute. Most coins have break in upper left corner of ZHONG 田 but some have faint suture instead, and worn coins may not show suture. BAO with dots in 尔 small, distinct; left dot more or less linear; right dot teardrop shaped; both dots angled out, right more than left. BAO 貝 bars incomplete, usually centered but shifted left in some coins; 貝 legs small, asymmetrical, left leg angular, acute, touching outer rim or nearly so; right leg smaller, club-like, pointing toward corner of inner rim but not touching. Some coins have break or constriction in the upper right side of BAO cap. Rev. inner rim narrow.

86 - Fields as in 85; characters larger, taller. YUAN left leg clearly touching outer rim; right leg constricted at origin from main bar, thickened at base. Rev. inner rim wider.

87 - Fields slightly smaller than in 85. QIAN 日 with large break in upper left corner; upper right corner acute. Left leg of YUAN angular, though this may be casting defect. BAO 貝 legs markedly asymmetrical.

88 - Obv. field similar to 87, reverse slightly smaller; characters tilted to right. YUAN left leg merging with outer rim. BAO 貝 legs markedly asymmetrical.

89 - Obv. field as in 87, rev. field markedly smaller, rev. outer rim wide. Bars in BAO 貝 shifted left; legs highly asymmetrical.

90 - Obv. field as in 87, rev. slightly smaller. QIAN head thick, erect, with thin, horizontal nose in middle. ZHONG 田 scarcely tapering, with small break in upper-left corner.

91 - Fields as in 89; no break in 田 upper left corner. QIAN with short head, nose close to outer rim, angled up; right side of horizontal stroke of 十 detached. YUAN left leg clearly reaching outer rim. BAO legs as in 85. Rev. inner rim moderately wide.

92 - Fields as in 85; flan larger, thicker, asymmetrical. QIAN 日 with bar complete; QIAN 十 tilted to right, with thick vertical stroke. ZHONG 田 close to inner rim. BAO 貝 with bars long, nearly complete.

93 - Fields similar to 85. Characters thin. Outer rims moderately narrow. YUAN right leg angular, segments straight.

94 - Fields similar to 85. YUAN left leg long; right leg with base flat on bottom, meeting rim at turn of barb. ZHONG bar 1 with left side thin, tapering; ZHONG base not meeting outer rim. BAO 貝 legs small, nearly symmetrical, right slightly thinner then left, neither reaching adjacent rim.

95 - Fields as in 85. Quite similar to 94. QIAN 乙 with small barb. YUAN left leg meeting rim at lower angle. ZHONG not touching inner rim, head not curved. Left leg of BAO 貝 angled down.

96 - Fields as in 85. Similar to 95. Differs in having narrower obv. outer rim. QIAN 日 with conspicuous sharp spine on upper left corner, longer barb on 乙. BAO bars long, incomplete, connecting left.

97 - Fields slightly larger than in 85. Very similar to 96, but characters thin. QIAN 日 lacking sharp spine on upper left corner. ZHONG head small, thin. BAO 貝 with bars short, centered; legs small, tapering, acute, neither reaching adjacent rim.

85	86	87	88	89	90
23.4–24.4 mm	23.9 mm	23.3 mm	23.6 mm	23.5 mm	23.5 mm
16	1	1	1	1	1

255   749   909   910   751   918

91	92	93	94	95	96
23.6–23.7 mm	24.5 x 25.0 mm	24.0 mm	23.9–24.5 mm	24.6 mm	24.3 mm
2	1	1	5	1	1

919   11-B   11-C   696   699   135

98 - Obv. field somewhat larger than in 97, markedly larger than in 85. QIAN head with nose angled up. Left leg YUAN short, tightly curved, well raised from outer rim. ZHONG head long. BAO 田 touching inner rim; 貝 legs long, thin, each reaching adjacent rim.

97	98
24.1 mm	24.5 mm
1	1

620   943

99 - Fields as in 85; characters larger. QIAN head shorter, with long, horizontal nose close to outer rim; bar in 日 long, centered. YUAN left leg moderately long, raised from outer rim. ZHONG head moderately large. BAO legs thick, asymmetrical, both angled slightly up, left leg touching outer rim, right larger and lower, not touching inner rim.

100 - Obv. field as in 85, reverse markedly smaller, rev. outer rim wide. QIAN head large, with long nose near middle, angled up, close to rim; 日 with long bar connecting right. YUAN left leg meeting outer rim nearly horizontally; right leg with narrow base. ZHONG head moderately large; 田 touching inner rim. BAO with tiny head on cap; 尔 with left dot unusually long, reaching top of 貝; 貝 legs symmetrical, angular, long, thin, acute, horizontal, each connecting to adjacent rim. Rev. inner rim moderately wide.

The next 13 vars (101–113) have left leg of YUAN long, more or less straight toward end and contacting or merging with outer rim. Six vars (108–113) have break in top of upper left quadrant of ZHONG 田; 108–111 also have constriction or break in right side of BAO cap, evident in unworn coins.

101 - Fields similar to 85. QIAN head with nose in middle, horizontal; top of 乙 with enlarged bulb. YUAN main bar with only slight hook; left leg long, clearly merging with outer rim at low angle. ZHONG head moderately large; base of ZHONG not reaching inner rim; right side of base constricted or detached. BAO with right side of cap short, nearly vertical, not touching inner rim. BAO legs horizontal; left leg long, merging with outer rim; right leg shorter, not reaching inner rim. Rev. inner rim moderately wide.

102 - Fields similar to 85. QIAN head with long nose in middle. Left leg YUAN long, straight and thinning toward end, reaching outer rim. BAO legs relatively thick, curved, nearly symmetrical, right merging with inner rim, left nearly reaching outer rim.

103 - Obv. field somewhat larger than in 85, rev. field as in 85. QIAN head strongly back curved, with nose in middle, horizontal; bar in 日 long, incomplete. YUAN with only slight hook on main bar; left leg long, tapering toward end, touching outer rim; right leg with narrow base broadly touching outer rim. ZHONG head smaller than in previous three vars, wedge-shaped; 田 scarcely tapering; left side of bar 2 detached. BAO 貝 bars long, shifted left; legs asymmetrical, left thicker and not touching outer rim, right thin and touching inner rim.

104 - Fields similar to 103. QIAN head strongly back-curved; nose close to outer rim. YUAN main bar with only slight hook. ZHONG head thin; 田 tapering on sides, close to inner rim; bar 2 not detached on left. Bars in BAO 貝 shifted left.

105 - Fields similar to 103. Characters thin. QIAN head strongly back-curved, nose in middle, angled up; QIAN 乙 angular between shaft and base; bars in QIAN 日 and BAO 貝 short, centered; left leg YUAN slightly raised from outer rim. Rubbed coin has break in top left of BAO cap.

106 - Small flan, fields, characters. QIAN head small, nose above middle, angled up; 日 bar incomplete, shifted right. YUAN left leg long, straight toward end, meeting outer rim. BAO legs small, neither quite touching adjacent rim.

107 - Obv. field as in 106, rev. field markedly larger. Characters tilted to left. QIAN head with nose near top, angled up; 日 bar incomplete. ZHONG head long; 田 asymmetrical, taller on right than on left. BAO legs horizontal, each touching adjacent rim.

108 - Field sizes similar to 85. QIAN head with nose near middle, slightly angled up. YUAN left leg long, merging with outer rim; right leg with bend forming nearly right angle, touching outer rim at turn of barb in unworn coins. ZHONG with moderately thick head in two coins, thinner in two coins; break in top of upper

99	100	101	102	103	104
24.0 mm	24.2 mm	23.5–24.1 mm	23.4 mm	24.2–24.3 mm	24.3 mm
1	1	2	1	2	1
298	1035	917	509	465-r2	263

105	106	107	108	109	110
24.5 mm	23.5 mm	23.9 mm	23.7–24.2 mm	24.2 mm	24.3 mm
1	1	1	4	1	1
263-r2	709	277	273-r2	684	461

left quadrant of 田 (all four coins show this). BAO cap with break or constriction in right side; 貝 legs horizontal, nearly symmetrical, each just touching adjacent rim or nearly so.

109 - Similar to 108, but fields larger (obv. field as in 74 above, rev. larger). Obv. inner rim thick. YUAN left leg long, merging with outer rim; right leg meeting rim at turn of barb. ZHONG head as in 108; break in top of upper left 田 quadrant, as in 108. BAO cap with short left side, not meeting outer rim; head small; BAO legs nearly symmetrical, horizontal, each nearly touching adjacent rim.

110 - Fields similar to 109. QIAN head tall, strongly back-curved, encroaching into outer rim, which is partly cut away; nose short, thin; 日 bar connecting to right. BAO with head on cap larger than in 109; 貝 legs relatively large, asymmetrical, left tapering, reaching outer rim, right thicker, just touching inner rim.

111 - Fields as in 109; characters similar. QIAN head shorter. Upper right corners of QIAN 日 and ZHONG 田 acute. YUAN right leg with narrower base. BAO with 貝 bars shifted left; legs smaller, acute, asymmetrical; right leg larger than left, horizontal, left leg angled down, each nearly touching adjacent rim.

112 - Fields similar to 109. QIAN head with nose in middle, thin, angled up; 日 clearly tapering on left side (in 109–111 of similar field sizes, 日 squared on left or nearly so, tapering on right). ZHONG head thin, triangular. YUAN right leg less vertical. BAO 貝 with bars shifted left; legs small, acute, asymmetrical, right leg reaching lower than left.

113 - Almost identical to 112; field sizes same. QIAN head thicker, with nose more horizontal; 日 with long bar, shifted left. YUAN left leg clearly merging with outer rim; right leg with smaller barb.

114 - Fields slightly smaller than in 85; outer rims moderately wide. Characters thick. Upper right corners of QIAN 日 and ZHONG 田 acute. QIAN head short, nose close to outer rim; 日 bar connected right. YUAN left leg long, meeting outer rim almost horizontally; right leg deeply curved. ZHONG base extending to below lower-right corner of inner rim; curving upward. BAO with bars in 貝 complete or nearly so; legs relatively large, nearly symmetrical, not angular, curving slightly upward, each meeting adjacent rim. Rubbed coin worn.

115 - Field sizes as in 85. QIAN head large, short, with long nose angled slightly up; 日 bar long, centered. YUAN left leg deeply curved, just reaching rim at low angle; right leg with base flat, meeting rim at turn of barb. ZHONG with large head, straight base. BAO cap with large head; 貝 bars centered; legs large, horizontal, asymmetrical, left leg smaller, acute, connecting with outer rim, right leg blunt, nearly reaching inner rim.

116 - Fields large, similar to 74; obv. field symmetrical; rev. asymmetrical, oblong. QIAN, BAO bars incomplete. QIAN with small head, nose close to outer rim, slightly angled up. YUAN left leg just touching outer rim, right leg incised from rim. ZHONG with large head; 田 asymmetrical, right side taller than left; ZHONG base curving down. BAO 貝 asymmetrical, right side taller than left, bars long, incomplete; legs angular, markedly asymmetrical, left longer, thicker, each leg just touching adjacent rim.

117 - Fields slightly smaller than in 85, rev. inner rim wide. Characters similar to 85, but QIAN nose angled slightly up; left leg YUAN longer, merging with outer rim nearly horizontally; right leg touching outer rim at turn of barb; no break in ZHONG 田; BAO 貝 legs thin, curved, nearly symmetrical, horizontally directed, not touching inner or outer rims.

118 - Obv. field as in 117, rev. field smaller; outer rims wider, esp. rev. All characters tilted slightly to right. QIAN with base of 乙 angled sharply downward. Left leg YUAN similar; right leg slightly recurved, with base broadly touching rim.

119 - Fields similar to 117. Characters thin; obv. outer rim moderately narrow. QIAN head small. Right leg YUAN with base rounded, incised from outer rim. ZHONG head thin. BAO legs small, nearly symmetrical.

120 - Fields similar to 117. YUAN right leg with narrow base. ZHONG with thick head; central vertical stroke curved to right; base curved. BAO 貝 bars shifted left; 王 and 尒 relatively large.

In next 13 vars (121–133), bars in BAO 貝 tapering from left to right, appearing angled down or actually angled down (see "g" under "BAO 目 bars", p. 23); 目 often slightly trapezoidal, longer on right side than on left.

111	112	113	114	115	116
23.9 mm	24.5 mm	24.1 mm	24.0 mm	23.7–24.5 mm	24.6 mm
1	1	1	1	2	1

692	1017	1018	613	689	462

117	118	119	120	121	122
23.8–24.0 mm	24.0 mm	23.5 mm	23.5 mm	23.4 mm	23.3–24.0 mm
2	1	1	1	1	6

263-A	710	595	615	921	147-r2

121 - Fields similar to 117. QIAN head with nose above middle, horizontal; 日 bar long, incomplete, centered. YUAN left leg moderately long, reaching outer rim. ZHONG head long, thin. BAO cap with acute right shoulder; dots in 尔 large, teardrop shaped, right dot meeting inner rim; 貝 with small, sharp spine on upper left corner; bars horizontal, centered, slightly tapering to right. BAO legs horizontal, asymmetrical, left leg thinner, tapering, right leg thicker, blunt; each leg touching adjacent rim. Rev. inner rim narrow. Rubbed coin with roseate hole.

122 - Fields similar to 117. QIAN head above middle, close to outer rim, angled slightly up; 日 tapering on both sides, bar long, nearly reaching each side. YUAN left leg long, straight toward end, merging with outer rim; right leg evenly curved, with relatively narrow base broadly contacting outer rim. ZHONG head thin; both sides 田 tapering. BAO legs small, thin, horizontal; asymmetrical, left longer and reaching outer rim, right not quite reaching inner rim.

123 - Fields somewhat smaller than in 117. QIAN head with thick nose close to outer rim. BAO 尔 unusual, with left dot elongate, touching top of 貝, right dot touching inner rim; 貝 legs asymmetrical, left longer, meeting outer rim, right small, angled down, close to corner of inner rim.

124 - Fields similar to 117. Characters thin; outer rims moderately wide. QIAN tall; head small, with thin, horizontal nose near middle. YUAN left leg just touching outer rim at low angle; right leg smoothly curved and incised from outer rim. ZHONG head thin; right side of 田 with large break in rubbed coin. BAO cap with break in right side; 貝 legs as in 123. Rev. inner rim narrow.

125 - Obv. field as in 117, rev. somewhat smaller. QIAN tall, as in 124; head small, nose near middle, angled up. YUAN left leg long, thin, straight toward end, merging with outer rim; right leg evenly curved, meeting outer rim near turn of barb. Left side ZHONG 田 squared. BAO legs small, nearly symmetrical, curved, neither leg reaching adjacent rim. Rev. inner rim moderately wide.

126 - Fields similar to 117. QIAN head short, with blunt nose near middle. YUAN left leg relatively short, just touching outer rim; right leg long, graceful, with thick, wide base broadly touching rim, barb short. ZHONG head narrow, linear. BAO legs as in 124. Rubbed coin has "nail mark" on reverse.

127 - Fields as in 117; characters tilted slightly to right. QIAN head short, with nose close to outer rim. YUAN left leg as in 126, meeting outer rim at low angle; right leg with base flattened on bottom, meeting outer rim near turn of barb. BAO with constriction in right side of cap; 貝 legs similar to those in 124.

128 - Fields similar to 117. Characters tilted to right. Compared to 127, QIAN 乙 with wider base. YUAN left leg long, straight toward end, touching outer rim; right leg with relatively narrow base. ZHONG head relatively thick; right side of bar 1 detached. BAO with dots in 尔 long; 貝 legs large, left leg longer and angular, right leg curved, each meeting adjacent rim.

129 - Fields similar to 117. Characters tilted slightly to right. QIAN head with nose above middle, horizontal. YUAN with left leg long, straight toward end, merging with outer rim at relatively large angle, as in 125; top bar at angle to main bar. ZHONG head thin, horizontal. BAO cap with upper right shoulder swollen, next to small break in top; 貝 legs similar to those in 127 and some others.

130 - Fields slightly larger than in 117. QIAN head with nose near middle, horizontal. YUAN left leg just touching outer rim, right leg meeting rim at turn of barb. Left side ZHONG 田 squared, right side strongly tapering. BAO cap with constriction in right side. BAO legs as in 127 and some others.

131 - Fields slightly larger than in 130, markedly larger than in 117. QIAN head tall, nose above middle, slightly angled up; left side of 日 nearly squared; 十 not connected to inner rim. ZHONG 田 scarcely tapering. BAO legs as in 130 and some others.

132 - Fields as in 130. Characters relatively thick. This and 133 have relatively thick obv. inner rim. QIAN head with nose near middle, angled up; 日 with bar short, shifted left. Right side 十 horizontal stroke detached. ZHONG 田 deep, both sides tapering. BAO legs as in 130, but heavier, right leg nearly touching inner rim.

133 - Fields similar to 131. QIAN head with nose close to outer rim; left side 日 scarcely tapering, bar tilted from horizontal. YUAN left leg long, straight toward end, merging with outer rim at relatively high angle. ZHONG 田 squared on left side, strongly tapering on right. BAO legs markedly asymmetrical, left leg much larger, thicker than right

123	**124**	**125**	**126**	**127**	**128**
23.5–23.7 mm	24.4 mm	23.1-24.2 mm	23.7 mm	23.5–23.8 mm	23.8 mm
2	1	3	1	2	1
33-r2	915	1086	268	975	912

129	**130**	**131**	**132**	**133**	
23.3–23.4 mm	24.1 mm	24.5 mm	23.6 mm	24.5 mm	
2	1	1	1	1	
247	303	731	1088	914	

134 - Fields as in 85 above. QIAN head large, nose above middle, angled up. YUAN with slightly recurved right leg, broadly touching outer rim. ZHONG 田 with both upper corners acute. BAO with vertical stroke in 尔 detached, becoming third dot; 貝 legs angular, highly asymmetrical, left much larger than right; each reaching adjacent rim.

135 - Fields similar to 85. QIAN tall, head small, with short nose angled upward. YUAN left leg long, straight toward end, just touching outer rim; right leg evenly curved, base narrow, broadly touching outer rim. ZHONG head small; left side of 田 squared. BAO with bars connecting left; 貝 legs thin, angular, nearly symmetrical, directed horizontally, left touching outer rim, right not touching inner rim. Rev. inner rim narrow.

136 - Fields similar to 85. QIAN head with long, horizontal nose; bar in 日 tilted from horizontal; bulb on shaft of 乙 enlarged, circular. YUAN with long left leg, straight toward end, just touching outer rim; right leg smoothly curved, with narrow base, as in 135. ZHONG head moderately large; left side 田 scarcely tapering. BAO 尔 with vertical stroke and dot forming inverted V; 貝 legs horizontal, markedly asymmetrical, left thicker than right, neither leg touching adjacent rim. Rev. inner rim moderately wide.

137 - Field sizes similar to 85, characters similar to 136. QIAN with heavier head, nose long, above middle, angled up; bar in 日 horizontal. YUAN left leg longer, nearly straight toward end, merging with outer rim; right leg broader along base, with larger barb. ZHONG head thinner, more strongly tapering on right side. BAO 尔 with vertical stroke and dot forming inverted V; 貝 legs similar to 136, but truncate rather than acute; left larger than right, neither touching adjacent rim.

138 - Fields similar to 85. QIAN tall, thin, nose slightly above middle, slightly angled up; 日 bar short, incomplete, shifted right. YUAN left leg deeply curved, with end directed horizontally and raised from or just touching but not merging with outer rim. YUAN right leg with sharp bend; base broad, more or less flat, reaching rim only at turn of barb. ZHONG head small; 田 slightly taller on right side than on left. BAO 尔 with small, more or less linear dots, left dot vertical, right dot somewhat thicker, angled out; 貝 with bars short, incomplete; legs small, nearly symmetrical, but right leg usually somewhat larger and lower than left, neither leg reaching adjacent rim. Roughly 3/4 of coins have break or constriction in upper right side of BAO cap. This var. resembles 85 and associated vars above, but differs in left leg of YUAN approaching rim nearly horizontally, in BAO legs not meeting the adjacent rims, and in having the left dot in 尔 vertical.

139 - Fields, characters similar to 138, but QIAN head with thick nose close to outer rim; ZHONG 田 deeper. Hole distorted; characters tilted slightly to right.

140 - Similar to 138, but fields somewhat larger, esp. rev.; outer rims narrow.

141 - Fields as in 140. QIAN head with nose in middle, angled up; base of 乙 narrow, rounded. YUAN left leg just touching outer rim at low angle; base of right leg flattened on bottom, incised from outer rim. ZHONG base straight. BAO 尔 with dots angled out; 貝 legs asymmetrical, rounded, left thicker than right, neither leg meeting adjacent rim.

142 - Fields larger than in 140; outer rims narrow. Characters similar to 141. Nose of QIAN head near middle, angled up; bulb on 乙 elongate, tapering. YUAN tall, with larger hook on main bar. ZHONG head long, thin; bars 1 and 2 incised from inner rim. Dots in BAO 尔 vertical; 貝 legs widely separated, thin, asymmetrical, both angled down, right smaller, neither touching adjacent rim.

143 - Obv. field as in 142, rev. field somewhat smaller. Characters thin. QIAN head with nose near middle, slightly angled up. YUAN tall, as in 142; left leg less deeply curved, approaching outer rim at higher angle;

134	135	136	137	138	139
24.4 mm	24.5 mm	23.7–24.2 mm	24.2 mm	23.3–24.2 mm	23.3 mm
1	1	2	1	12	1

265	463	565	1065	486	1023

140	141	142	143	144	145
23.9 mm	25.1 mm	24.7 mm	25.0 mm	25.0 mm	25.1 mm
1	1	1	1	1	1

728	685	741	693	1060	563

right leg smoothly curved, base narrow, broadly meeting outer rim; main bar YUAN tilted down to right. BAO 尔 with both dots linear, angled out, right more than left. 貝 legs horizontal, asymmetrical, left leg much longer than right and touching outer rim, right leg not touching inner rim.

144 - Fields similar to 143. QIAN with bar in 日 long, incomplete; head short, with long, thick, horizontal nose close to outer rim; base of 乙 distinctly angled down. YUAN left leg reaching outer rim at high angle. ZHONG head small. BAO 貝 bars complete or nearly so; legs large, angular, thick, asymmetrical; left leg angled down, not meeting outer rim; right leg larger, horizontal, reaching inner rim.

145 - Fields as in 141. Rubbed coin crudely cast, with gaps in parts of characters. QIAN head with nose near middle, angled up, touching outer rim. YUAN left leg slightly recurved; right leg evenly curved, base broadly meeting rim. Left side of BAO cap short; 貝 legs long, thin, curved, merging with inner and outer rims; bars in 目 long, nearly complete; dots in 尔 angled. [With the slightly recurved left leg YUAN and thin, curved BAO 貝 legs, this var. probably fits better in the Prancing Yuan group (p. 58), though the strongly angled nose on the QIAN head is unusual for that group.]

146 - Fields slightly larger than in 141, characters thin. QIAN head tall, with long horizontal nose above middle; base of 乙 right-angled, with small barb. YUAN left leg meeting rim nearly horizontally; right leg evenly curved, base narrow, rounded, meeting rim at turn of barb. ZHONG not touching inner rim. BAO cap narrow, with symmetrical shoulders and break in right side, left side free from outer rim; 貝 legs thin, angular, tapering, right leg lower, each just touching adjacent rim. [171–177, p. 56, also have left side BAO cap free from outer rim.]

147 - Coin asymmetrical; minimum obv. and maximum rev. field diameters as in 146. QIAN head with thin nose in middle; base of 乙 angular; left side 日 scarcely tapering. YUAN left leg shallowly curved, raised from rim; right leg meeting rim at turn of barb. ZHONG bars 1, 2 reaching inner rim. BAO with left side of cap incised from outer rim; 貝 legs asymmetrical, left thicker, neither meeting adjacent rim.

148 - Fields similar to 146. QIAN head short, not reaching outer rim. YUAN left leg barely touching outer rim, at low angle. ZHONG not touching inner rim; head damaged in rubbed coin; appears to be thin as in 147. BAO cap asymmetrical, angle of left shoulder greater than right. BAO with dots in 尔 both strongly angled out; 貝 legs short, curved, thin, nearly symmetrical, each well separate from adjacent rim.

149 - Fields similar to 146. QIAN, BAO bars long, centered. QIAN head relatively large, with nose above middle, angled up. YUAN main bar with bulbous hook; end of left leg nearly horizontal; right leg sharply bent, just touching outer rim at turn of barb, base flat. ZHONG not touching inner rim. BAO legs asymmetrical, right larger and nearly meeting inner rim, left thin, angled down, not meeting outer rim.

150 - Fields similar to 85 above. QIAN head erect, nearly straight, horizontal nose above middle; 日 strongly tapering on both sides. YUAN left leg straight toward end, merging with outer rim at relatively high angle; right leg evenly curved, broadly merging with outer rim. ZHONG with moderately large head; bar 1 not touching outer rim; 田 tapering on both sides, with upper corners acute. BAO legs asymmetrical, angular; left leg twice as long as right, meeting outer rim; right incised from inner rim. Rev. inner rim moderately wide.

151 - Fields as in 150. Characters thin. QIAN head small, nose short, above middle, angled up; accessory spine at base of head. ZHONG bar 1 not touching outer rim; 田 with small break at upper right corner.

152 - Fields as in 150; flan smaller, outer rims narrower. In 152, YUAN left leg less sharply bent, right leg with shallower curve, narrow base, meeting outer rim at turn of barb. ZHONG bar 1 reaching outer rim, BAO 尔 markedly smaller.

153 - Fields similar to 150. QIAN head large. Obv. inner rim relatively thick. YUAN with long left leg reaching outer rim horizontally, right leg sharply bent, touching outer rim only at turn of barb; barb short, blunt. ZHONG head relatively short, thick. BAO legs as in 150, but right leg heavier.

154 - Fields as in 150. QIAN head small, nose thin, horizontal. YUAN left leg long, merging with outer rim at low angle; right leg with sharp bend, base wide, flat, incised from outer rim, meeting at turn of barb. ZHONG head moderately thick; 田 slightly tapering on both sides. Right side of BAO cap short, nearly vertical, not touching inner rim; 貝 legs moderately heavy, left longer than right. Upper corners of QIAN 日 and ZHONG 田 acute on both sides. Coin with smaller flan has narrower obv. and rev. outer rims.

155 - Fields as in 153. Characters similar to 154. Coin thick (1.6 mm), characters thin. YUAN left leg less deeply curved than in 154; right leg with base flat, incised from outer rim. ZHONG head thin. BAO cap with small head; 尔 dots thin, linear. As in 154, right side of cap nearly vertical and not touching inner rim. Quite similar to Yoshida's Y134U, but fields slightly larger in 155.

146	147	148	149	150	151
24.5 mm	23.8 x 24.5 mm	24.4 mm	24.8 mm	24.2–24.3 mm	24.1 mm
1	1	1	1	2	1

131	1036	11	11-cr	147	147-A

152	153	154		155		156	157
23.4 mm	24.1 mm	23.8–24.4 mm		24.7 mm		24.6 mm	24.3 mm
1	1	2	Y134L	1	Y134U	1	1

147-A-r2	464	708	1053	719	304

156 - Obv. field similar to 150, rev. clearly larger. QIAN head with horizontal nose near middle. YUAN left leg similar to 155, right leg with curved base, not flat. ZHONG head long; 田 not tapering. BAO cap leaning slightly to right; 貝 legs tapering, not angular; asymmetrical, left longer, touching outer rim; right tiny, angled down, not touching inner rim.

157 - Fields similar to 150. QIAN head thick, with nose above middle. YUAN left leg just meeting outer rim at low angle; right leg recurved. ZHONG 田 slightly tapering. BAO cap tilted to right; left half of middle horizontal stroke of 王 broken away, drifting; 貝 legs angular, right larger, meeting inner rim, left not meeting outer rim.

158 - Fields similar to 150. QIAN head strongly curved, with nose above middle, angled up. YUAN left leg reaching outer rim nearly horizontally; right leg broadly contacting rim, slightly recurved. ZHONG head small; bar 1 incised from inner and outer rims. BAO legs asymmetrical but reversed from 157, left longer and reaching outer rim, right not reaching inner rim.

158
24.4 mm
1

690

159 - Fields as in 150. Characters tilted slightly to right. QIAN head large, with nose near middle, slightly angled up. Left leg YUAN long, meeting rim at low angle, tip not fully merging with rim. ZHONG head large. BAO legs thick, asymmetrical, right larger, incised from inner rim; left tapering, meeting outer rim.

160 - Fields similar to 150. QIAN head with nose near middle, angled up. Both sides of ZHONG 田 markedly tapering; bar 2 thin, tapering and tilted up on left side. BAO 王 ladderlike, touching left side of cap; 貝 with bars shifted left; legs thick, blunt, angular, nearly symmetrical, left slightly thicker, neither leg quite touching adjacent rim.

The next five vars (161–165) are similar to one another, with the 乙 base relatively narrow and angled down. See also var. 170, in which 乙 has broader base.

161 - Fields slightly larger than in 150. QIAN head with nose in middle, horizontal. YUAN tall, left leg thin, acute at end, just reaching outer rim; right leg with about half of base touching rim. ZHONG head small; 田 with left side squared, right side markedly tapering; right side bar 2 longer than left. BAO 王 narrower at top, free from cap; 貝 bars centered; legs small, thin, horizontal, nearly symmetrical, neither touching adjacent rim.

162 - Fields similar to 150, somewhat smaller than in 161, rev. outer rim wider than in 161. Characters very similar to 161; base of YUAN right leg a little wider. BAO with 貝 bars thin, shifted left.

163 - Fields markedly smaller than in preceding two vars. QIAN head thick, erect, with short nose in middle. YUAN legs similar to 162. BAO legs asymmetrical, left thicker than right, neither reaching adjacent rim.

164 - Field sizes as in 150. QIAN head thin, nose near middle, slightly angled up; 乙 base narrow. YUAN left leg longer, more deeply curved than in preceding three vars. ZHONG 田 scarcely tapering. BAO legs large, thick, blunt, curved rather than angular; left leg smaller, incised from outer rim, right longer and thicker, merging with inner rim.

165 - Obv. field similar to 150, rev. field smaller. QIAN head with nose close to outer rim; 日 tapering more on right than on left. YUAN left leg reaching rim at relatively high angle. ZHONG bar 2 shorter on right. BAO legs similar to 164 but smaller, more angular. BAO 目 bars fused together just below center.

166 - Small flan, fields; rev. field unusually small, rev. outer rim wide. QIAN head short, slightly curved, long nose angled up; 日 squared on left side, bar long, nearly complete; 乙 barb thick. YUAN with long left leg merging with outer rim at low angle; right leg evenly curved. ZHONG 田 squared on left, tapering slightly on right. BAO legs asymmetrical, left thick, right tapering and acute, each touching adjacent rim.

167 - Coin asymmetrical; flan and hole broader than tall. QIAN head short, with nose long, horizontal, close to outer rim; bar in 日 nearly complete. YUAN with long left leg, straight toward end; right leg broadly contacting outer rim. ZHONG 田 with both sides only slightly tapering. BAO legs thin, acute, left larger than right, each reaching adjacent rim.

168 - Fields slightly larger than in 150; obv. and rev. outer rims moderately narrow. QIAN head curved, incised from outer rim, with nose in middle, horizontal. YUAN left leg long; straight, horizontal toward end; just touching outer rim; right leg evenly curved, meeting rim at turn of barb. BAO legs angular, blunt, asymmetrical, left longer than right, each incised from adjacent rim.

159	160	161	162	163	164
24.3 mm	24.2–24.5 mm	24.3–24.7 mm	24.5 mm	23.5 mm	24.5 mm
1	4	3	1 — Y135U	1	1

| 274 | 1087 | 745 | 686 | 913 | 267 |

165	166	167	168	169	170
24.1 mm	23.2 mm	24.0 x 24.9 mm	23.8 mm	23.3 mm	24.0 mm
1	1	1	1	1	1

| 1054 | 736 | 211 | 704 | 750 | 1048 |

169 - Fields slightly smaller than in 150. Obv. outer rim moderately narrow. QIAN, BAO bars long, complete or nearly so. QIAN head large, thick, with nose angled up, reaching outer rim. YUAN left leg moderately long, merging with outer rim; right leg meeting rim toward turn of barb. ZHONG head thick. BAO legs large, asymmetrical, left longer and meeting outer rim, right not reaching inner rim.

170 - Fields as in 150. Obv. and rev. outer rims moderately narrow. QIAN with bar in 日 nearly complete, connecting right; 乙 base angular. YUAN left leg deeply curved, touching outer rim at low angle; right leg with narrow base, half of base touching outer rim; barb large. ZHONG head moderately large. BAO cap with small head; bars in 貝 complete or nearly so, legs horizontal, right leg larger and thicker than left, each meeting adjacent rim.

The following seven vars have left side of BAO cap separate from outer rim (see also 146, 147, p. 52). In first five, left side of cap short and left leg of YUAN meeting outer rim horizontally or slightly recurved. In last two, left side of cap longer; left leg of YUAN acute, meeting outer rim at higher angle, just touching rim; characteristic break in middle horizontal stroke of ZHONG 田.

171 - Obv. field as in 150; rev. slightly larger. QIAN head with nose near middle, horizontal, tapering (nose tapering in next four vars as well); 日 bar long, shifted right. YUAN left leg long, evenly curved, touching outer rim nearly horizontally; right leg with flat base, meeting outer rim at turn of barb. ZHONG 田 with both sides tapering. BAO with left side of cap short, clearly separate from outer rim; head of cap large; 王 ladderlike, symmetrical; left dot in 尔 linear, right dot teardrop shaped; 貝 legs asymmetrical, left thicker than right, neither leg reaching adjacent rim.

172 - Like 171, but smaller rev. field, wider rev. inner rim. Characters nearly identical, but BAO 尔 with central vertical stroke truncated between dots; left leg BAO 貝 longer, reaching outer rim.

173 - Obv. field as in 171, rev. field smaller. Characters thin, obv. outer rim narrow. Right leg YUAN with narrow base. ZHONG 田 with small break on top near upper right corner. BAO with narrow head on cap; 貝 legs as in 172. Rev. inner rim narrow.

174 - Fields somewhat smaller than in 172; characters similar but smaller. ZHONG 田 tapering more strongly on right side than on left. BAO 貝 with right leg thicker than left; left leg reaching outer rim.

175 - Fields similar to 174. Outer rims relatively wide. QIAN head with nose in middle, slightly angled up. ZHONG 田 tapering roughly equally on both sides. BAO legs rounded, blunt, nearly symmetrical, neither leg touching adjacent rim.

176 - Fields as in 175. QIAN 日 with short, centered bar; head with horizontal nose. Left leg YUAN tapering toward end, meeting outer rim at high angle, incised from rim. Break in center horizontal stroke of ZHONG 田, separating left side of stroke from vertical stroke; in one coin, break on both sides of vertical stroke. Left side of BAO cap longer than in previous five vars, but not touching outer rim. BAO 尔 has left dot tiny, right dot large, elongate; 貝 legs slightly thicker than in 175, nearly symmetrical, rounded, left leg turned up, each leg close to but incised from adjacent rim.

177 - Fields markedly larger than in 176; 尔 dots and break in 田 as in 176. BAO with break in right side of cap; 貝 legs markedly asymmetrical; left leg angular, much longer and thicker than right and meeting outer rim; right curved, not meeting inner rim.

Addendum to this group - See entry 454, p. 109.

171	172	173	174	175	176
24.4–24.5 mm	23.7 mm	24.5 mm	22.9 mm	24.3 mm	24.1–24.5 mm
2	1	1	1	1	4
687	561	1027	491	490	279

177					
24.2 mm					
1					
618					

WIDE CHARACTERS, PRANCING YUAN
(濶字挑元, *katsu ji chô gen*)

This group is similar to the preceding Wide Characters group, but differs in having the left leg of YUAN long and recurved along the outer rim. The BAO 貝 legs are long, often thin and curved rather than angular, more or less horizontally directed, and with few exceptions reach the adjacent inner and outer rims. Four broad groups of field sizes are evident: 1) 179 and related coins, with the largest fields, and flan size usually over 25.0 mm; 2) 188 and related coins, with somewhat smaller fields, and flan size often over 25.0 mm; 3) common vars 211 and 219 and related coins, with field sizes somewhat smaller than in 188 and markedly smaller than in 179, and flan size less than 25.0 mm; and 4) several varieties (most of them placed toward the end of the section) with field sizes smaller than in 211/219, and with flan size usually less than 24.0 mm and in some cases less than 23.0 mm. In identification, field sizes and to some extent flan size can place a coin into one of the categories above, eliminating various other possibilities. A useful way to proceed after that is to pay attention to the degree to which the left leg of YUAN contacts the outer rim. This group includes some of the most abundant varieties of QYZB (see the QUICK ID, pp. 24–25); 63% of all coins in this group found in bulk lots will be either 211 (35%) or 219 (28%). Doo (2003: p. 95) illustrates six coins in this group (diameter 24.4–25.9 mm) and lists them as "Valued 10," but does not explain why he considers them as other than value-1. Yoshida numbers eight plain-reverse varieties and three with reverse mark, the latter being uncommon, and noted that there is much subtle variation among coins. This complex group needs further study.

178 - Large flan, small fields, wide outer rims. QIAN with bar in 貝 complete. ZHONG with large head and markedly curved base. YUAN short. Bars in BAO 貝 appear shifted or connected left; legs large.

179 - Large flan, fields. QIAN with 日 bar incomplete, centered or shifted right; QIAN head with nose near middle, slightly angled up. Dots in 尔 thick; linear, teardrop, or wedge shaped; right dot thicker than left; both angled out. Left leg of YUAN moderately recurved, appressed to outer rim for some distance near end. ZHONG head moderately large. BAO 貝 bars long, incomplete, centered in reduced space with rounded inside corners. About 1/4 of coins have a constriction or break in right side of BAO cap.

180 - Similar to 179, but rev. field slightly larger, characters thinner. Hole slightly broader than tall. QIAN head smaller, ZHONG head thin. Bars in QIAN 日 and BAO 貝 short, centered. BAO cap with break in right side. YUAN left leg incised from outer rim; right leg mostly incised, meeting rim at turn of barb. BAO 王 characteristically has vertical stroke thin and below level of horizontal strokes. Dots in 尔 thin; 貝 legs thin. There is some question whether 179 simply represents worn examples of 180. Worn 180 have thicker characters and legs of YUAN merge with rim, appearing like 179, but bars in BAO 貝 remain in rectangular rather than oval space.

181 - Fields similar to 180; outer rims narrower. YUAN left leg longer, extending farther along outer rim. Zhong head intermediate between 179 and 180. Dots in BAO 尔 small.

182 - Fields similar to 179; outer rims narrower; hole broader than tall. Characters large, robust; long, nearly complete bars in QIAN 日 and BAO 貝; BAO 貝 wider.

183 - Similar to 180, but obv. field somewhat smaller. Hole slightly broader than tall. Coin thick, 1.8 mm. QIAN and ZHONG heads smaller than in 180. Break in upper right corner of QIAN 日 and also in right side of BAO cap. YUAN left leg contacting outer rim for only short distance; right leg slightly recurved. Dots in BAO 尔 quite small; BAO 貝 legs small; left leg not reaching outer rim. Reverse inner

178	179	180	181	182	183
25.5 mm	25.0–25.5 mm	24.6–25.5 mm	25.1 mm	24.7 x 25.1 mm	25.5 mm
1	Y141	12		24	Y139	1		1		1	
1029	829	15	15-D	15-B	845

184	185	186	187		
25.4 mm	25.5 mm	24.9–25.7 mm	25.1 mm		
1		1		11		1					
15-r2	1094	15A-r3	705		

rim narrower than in 180.

184 - Obv. field as in 179, rev. somewhat larger. QIAN head with nose slightly angled up, Bars in BAO 貝 connecting left.

185 - Fields as in 179. QIAN head small; bar in 日 long, connecting right; bars in BAO 貝 connecting left.

186 - Similar to 180. Obv. field as in 180, rev. field markedly smaller, rev. outer rim wider. Most coins have break in right side of BAO cap.

187 - Obv. field slightly smaller and rev. field markedly smaller than in 179; both fields smaller than in 186; rev. outer rim wide. QIAN head with nose near outer rim, angled up. YUAN left leg with sharp bend as it nears outer rim. ZHONG cramped, 正 close to inner and outer rims. BAO with head on cap large, wide; 貝 bars centered in reduced space.

188 - Obv. field consistently smaller than in 179; rev. as in 179 or slightly smaller. Field sizes intermediate between 179 and related coins above, and 211/219 and related coins below. QIAN with bar in 日 incomplete, usually shifted right; head with nose near center, horizontal or slightly angled up. YUAN left leg only slightly recurved, raised above outer rim or barely touching near the tip; right leg incised from outer rim. About 3/4 of coins have constriction or break in right side of BAO cap. BAO with dots in 尔 angled outward; bars in 貝 incomplete, usually shifted somewhat left; may appear connected left in worn coins. Var. 188 has same field sizes as Yoshida's Y140, but shows larger ZHONG head; in 188, BAO legs long and connecting to inner and outer rims. Possibly Yoshida's conception of common var. Y140 encompasses common var. 188 here. See also 189, 191, and 195.

189 - Obv. field as in 188, rev. slightly smaller. Outer rims relatively wide. Characters similar, but break near upper right corner QIAN 日; BAO 貝 legs markedly asymmetrical, left leg small, not reaching outer rim.

190 - Fields similar to 188. Left leg YUAN long, more like that in 179 above; middle horizontal stroke in ZHONG 田 incomplete on both sides.

191 - Fields as in 188; characters similar to 188, but with break in top of BAO 貝; right dot in 尔 curved.

192 - Obv. field slightly smaller than in 188. QIAN head with nose above middle, angled up. ZHONG 田 with small spine on upper right corner; unusual break in right side. Left leg YUAN tightly recurved. Upper right corner of BAO 貝 with small spine (compare with 203 below).

193 - Fields as in 188. QIAN 日 bar incomplete; center or shifted right. Left leg YUAN strongly recurved, similar to that in 190; right leg not markedly recurved, which separates it from 198 below. BAO 貝 with bars incomplete, center or shifted left; 尔 dots angled outwards. About half of coins have constriction or break in the right side of the BAO cap.

194 - Field sizes as in 188; characters similar; differs in BAO 尔 having exaggerated, conspicuously curved dots.

195 - Fields as in 188. Similar to 188, but characters thin. ZHONG head thinner. BAO 貝 legs asymmetrical, left longer than right; right leg not meeting inner rim. Compare with 208 below, which has different reverse side.

196 - Small flan. Obv. field as in 188, rev. smaller. Obv. outer rim variable, moderately narrow to somewhat wider. QIAN head small, nose in middle, slightly angled up; 日 bar shifted right. YUAN left leg as in 193. BAO 貝 bars centered. Compare with 208 below.

197 - Coin, fields asymmetrical; minimum field diameters as in 188. QIAN tilted to left; bar in 日 nearly complete, head short with long nose near base. YUAN left leg shallowly curved, touching outer rim near end; base of right leg broadly merging with rim. ZHONG head thin. BAO with wide cap; head large; bars in 貝 nearly complete, connecting left.

198 - Fields similar to 188. Characters thin in less-worn coins. QIAN head small, strongly back-curved, incised from outer rim (several coins have rim trimmed away slightly around top of head), with nose above middle; bar in 日 incomplete, shifted right. YUAN left leg long; right leg markedly recurved, incised from outer rim. ZHONG head thin. BAO 貝 bars short, centered. This and next two vars are similar, with slightly different field sizes and rim widths. ZHONG head in rubbed coin unusually thin; others somewhat thicker. For another, closely related var., see 455 under 'Addenda' at end of catalog.

199 - Fields slightly smaller than in 198; flan smaller. One coin unusually thick, 1.8 mm.

188	189	190	191	192	193
24.5–25.7 mm	25.1 mm	25.1 mm	25.0–25.4 mm	24.7 mm	24.6–25.7 mm
29 · cf. Y140	1 · Y140L	1	2	1	22

| 837 | 839 | 984 | 854 | 1068 | 1067 |

194	195	196	197	198	199
24.5 mm	24.3–24.8 mm	23.3–23.8 mm	25.4 x 25.7 mm	24.9–25.2 mm	23.3–24.2 mm
1	2 · Y140U	11	1	13	2

| 826 | 814 | 840 | 726 | 9H | 813 |

200 - Obv. field similar to 188, rev. larger. QIAN head with nose above middle, close to outer rim. Outer rims narrower than in 188.

201 - Obv. field slightly larger than in 188, rev. similar. Characters thin. QIAN head small, thin; 日 scarcely tapering. YUAN right leg with tall, acute barb. Right side of ZHONG 田 squared, left scarcely tapering. Horizontal stroke in BAO 尔 not joining cap on right side; rev. outer rim moderately wide.

202 - Fields similar to 188. ZHONG 田 cramped, touching inner and outer rims. BAO 尔 unusually small; large break in top of 貝.

200	201	202
25.0 mm	25.5 mm	24.8 mm
1	1	1

| 667 | 848 | 15C |

203 - Obv. field similar to 188, rev. field larger; outer rims and rev. inner rim relatively narrow. ZHONG 田 with small spine on upper right corner. BAO 貝 narrow, with small, sharp spine projecting upward from upper right corner, reaching bottom of 尔 (compare with 192 above).

204 - Fields similar to 188. Characters similar, except left side of ZHONG 田 continues down to merge with bar 2. Left leg YUAN long, meeting outer rim for 1/3 its length.

205 - Obv. fields similar to 188, rev. somewhat smaller. QIAN head with nose angled up, close to outer rim. YUAN left leg deeply curved. BAO 尔 with left dot vertical; in some coins, 貝 with swollen upper right corner and suture, as in 219 below; bars long, incomplete, usually shifted left.

206 - Fields similar to 188; hole slightly broader than tall; obv. inner rim thin. Characters similar to 205 (left dot in 尔 vertical), but thin; left leg YUAN longer, less deeply curved; break in upper right corner of ZHONG 田.

207 - Coin asymmetrical; obv. field asymmetrical, with minimum diameter as in 188; rev. field symmetrical, as in 188. Hole slightly broader than tall. QIAN 日, BAO 貝 with bars long, incomplete, centered. ZHONG head thin. Left dot in BAO 尔 close to vertical.

208 - Obv. field similar to 188; rev. field slightly larger, rev. inner and outer rims narrower. Characters thin.

209 - Small flan. Obv. field as in 188; outer rims and rev inner rim narrow. Characters similar to 208, but thicker; ZHONG head thick and wedge shaped rather than concave on top. BAO 貝 legs relatively thick.

210 - Flan thin, ≤1.0 mm; characters robust. Fields similar to 188. Obv. outer rim moderately narrow. QIAN 日 bar long, connected right, YUAN left leg long, appressed to outer rim for more than 1/3 its length. ZHONG head large. BAO 貝 bars incomplete, centered.

211 - Fields somewhat smaller than in 188. QIAN 日 with right side tapering more than left and with acute upper right corner, as in 188; bar long, incomplete, centered or shifted slightly right. QIAN head with nose near middle, angled up. YUAN left leg slightly more recurved than in 188, touching outer rim for a somewhat longer distance near end. ZHONG 田 wide, nearly touching inner and outer rims; with acute, sometimes spine-like, upper right corner. About 5% of coins have constriction or break in the right side of BAO cap. BAO with both dots in 尔 of angled outward; top bar of 王 tilted slightly downward to the right; bars in BAO 貝 connecting left, merging with left side, even in relatively unworn coins, rather than simply being shifted left, which is main difference from 188, aside from somewhat smaller fields.

212 - Fields similar to 188. Characters thin; similar to 188, with left leg YUAN just touching outer rim. Differs from 188 in having BAO 貝 bars connected left; unusual break in lower right side of 貝. Very similar to 223 below (except for break in 貝, which may be casting error); see description for 223.

213 - Fields similar to 188. Characters similar to 211, but 貝 bars shifted left rather than connecting left; sometimes touching left, but incised from side of 貝. Rubbed coin with break in left side of 貝, others not.

214 - Fields similar to 188. Characters small. Coin poorly cast. QIAN head small; bulb on 乙 shaft circular. YUAN left leg scarcely recurved, touching outer rim only at tip; right leg incised from rim. ZHONG bar 1 not meeting outer rim. BAO with dots in 尔 thin, both angled outward, with middle, vertical stroke missing; 貝 bars not clear in rubbed coin but at least top bar is long, complete. Similar to Yoshida's Y149U, but that var. has both sides QIAN 日 tapering, lacks circular bulb on 乙 shaft, and has wider rev. inner rim.

203	204	205	206	207	208
24.3 mm	25.0 mm	24.2–25.2 mm	24.4 mm	24.0 x 24.5 mm	24.7 mm
1	1	10	1	1	1 Y143

838	851	1090	1071	847	9-r12

209	210	211 #1	211 #2	212	213
23.5 mm	24.3–24.7 mm	24.0–24.7 mm		24.7 mm	24.0–24.8 mm
1	2	216		1	8

477	815	9-r8	9I-r2	9-r11	841

215 - Small flan; obv. field similar to 188, rev. somewhat smaller. Characters similar to 188, left leg YUAN just touching outer rim. ZHONG head large. Bars in BAO 貝 touching but slightly incised from left side (not connected).

216 - Small flan. Obv. field as in 188, rev. somewhat smaller. Similar to 196 in flan, field, character, and outer-rim sizes. QIAN head with long, horizontal nose near middle. YUAN left leg touching outer rim only at end; right leg thick, with unusually broad base. ZHONG head thicker than in 196. BAO 王 tall, narrow; 貝 with bars shifted left, not connected; legs small. Rubbed coin with roseate hole.

214	215	216
24.6 mm	23.5 mm	23.2 mm
1 cf. Y149U	1	1

9-R	987	831

217 - Obv. field slightly smaller, rev. markedly smaller than in 188. QIAN head with nose near middle, slightly angled up; 日 bar long, centered. YUAN left leg moderately recurved, touching rim for about 1/4 its length. ZHONG head thin. BAO with left side of 貝 concave, connecting to 王 (casting error?) at upper left corner; bars in 貝 thin, tapering, connected left; legs asymmetrical, left thicker than right, tilted up. Rev. inner rim wide.

218 - Fields similar to 217 (reverse worn, obscured). Characters similar to 217, but tilted slightly to right. QIAN 日 bar long, incomplete, shifted right. BAO 貝 legs thinner than in 217, left leg not tilted up.

219 - Fields similar to 211; somewhat smaller than in 188. Characters quite similar to 211 above. 219 differs from 211 in having left dot of BAO 尔 vertical and right dot angled outward; bars in BAO 貝 shifted left but not clearly connecting left (although they may appear connected in worn coins); and top bar of 王 horizontal or tilted slightly upward rather than downward to right. Bar in QIAN 日 long, incomplete, centered, often slightly tapering left to right. ZHONG bar 2 complete (219 #2) or incomplete, not reaching inner or outer rim, or either rim (219 #1). Among coins in this and next var., about 30% have break in top of BAO 貝 near right corner, with swelling to right of break; about 30% show only scarcely visible suture and/or swelling indicating where break should be; and 40% show no indication of break. Break in 貝 not seen in similar, common var. 211. Coins in some other vars occasionally show break in same position in 貝, so this feature alone is not diagnostic. A few coins of this variety have constriction or break in right side of BAO cap, a feature common in some other vars. 219 is about 80% as common as 211 above.

220 - Like 219, but characters thin; dots in 尔 smaller, thinner. ZHONG bar 2 clearly separate from inner and outer rims. Rubbed coin is largest example, 25.0 mm; smaller coins have narrower outer rims.

221 - Like 219, but BAO cap with pronounced, blunt projection on right shoulder. BAO 貝 with incomplete bars, usually long; centered or shifted left but not fused with left side. Most coins show break (or swelling or suture indicative of position of break) on top of BAO 貝 near right corner, as in 219. ZHONG head with swollen tip. Some coins placed in var. 219 show a slight projection on the BAO cap and/or a slightly enlarged tip of the ZHONG head, and so vars 219 and 221 may grade into one another.

222 - Fields similar to 188. QIAN head with nose near center, angled up. YUAN left leg scarcely recurved, reaching outer rim only at tip. ZHONG 田 taller on right side than on left; bar 2 not reaching inner or outer rim. BAO with left shoulder of cap rounded, impinging on top of 王, break in right side of cap; 尔 with both dots angled out. BAO 貝 legs unusually thin, each just touching adjacent rim.

223 - Fields similar to 211. Very similar to 212 above, characters similarly thin, same field sizes. BAO lacks break in lower right part of 貝 but instead has same break near upper right corner that is common in 211; 尔 with vertical stroke short and tiny dots angled out; 日 bars shifted left but not connected left. Rev. inner rim wider than in 212.

224 - Easily identified by the thick, cramped, ladder-like 王 in BAO. Fields as in 188 above. QIAN with bar in 日 short, centered; 乙 with sharp angle between shaft and base. ZHONG with thick central vertical stroke. BAO 尔 with left dot thin, slightly angled out; right dot heavy, triangular, markedly angled, touching inner rim; bars in 貝 short, centered. One coin has thinner characters than others.

225 - Obv. field as in 219; rev. smaller. Characters thick, tilted slightly to right. QIAN head short, horizontal nose nearly touching outer rim; bar in 日 long, centered. ZHONG head thin, rather uniform in thickness across length; 田 nearly rectangular, with small spine on upper right corner; bar 2 reaching inner rim, not reaching outer rim. BAO 貝 with small space containing nearly complete bars; top stroke of 王 angled down; left dot in 尔 vertical, right dot long, exaggerated, impinging on inner rim; 貝 legs thick. Mark near upper right corner of inner rim on reverse; unusual in position for bona-fide reverse mark but thicker than

217	218	219 #1	219 #2	220	221
23.8 mm	23.7–24.6 mm	23.7–24.6 mm		23.8–25.0 mm	23.7–24.7 mm
1	2	173 Y142L		10+	8 Y142U
666	820	9-r9	9-r2	9K-r2	9A-r2

222	223	224	225	226	227
23.7 mm	24.3 mm	24.0–24.7 mm	24.4 mm	23.8 mm	24.3 mm
1	1	20 Y148	1	1	2
600	1070	9G-r3	844	9B-r2	9-r16

228
24.2 mm
1
9M

typical for nail mark.

226 - Field sizes as in 225. Characters similar, but not tilted. QIAN head with nose near middle, angled up. ZHONG with 田 tapering on both sides and lacking spine; bar 2 just touching outer rim, not reaching inner rim. BAO 尔 with left dot vertical; 貝 bars shifted left in normal space.

227 - Fields as in 225. Similar to 225 but characters not tilted. YUAN left leg less strongly recurved. ZHONG head more markedly curved. BAO cap with large head; left dot in 尔 thick, vertical, right dot triangular, touching inner rim; 貝 bars long, nearly centered in normal space; rev. inner and outer rims relatively wide.

228 - Obv. field as in 225, rev. somewhat smaller. QIAN head with nose near top; 日 bar nearly complete (rubbed coin worn). YUAN left leg broadly appressed to outer rim. ZHONG head thick. BAO with 尔 dots angled out; bars in 貝 centered.

229 - Obv. field slightly smaller than in 228, rev. markedly smaller, rev. inner rim unusually wide, almost reaching outer rim.

230 - Fields similar to 229. Hole small. QIAN head thin, with nose close to outer rim; bar in 日 centered in oval space. Compared to 229, YUAN left leg shorter, less recurved; right leg with taller, narrower barb. ZHONG head with tip detached (error?). Head on BAO cap tall, narrow, acute; 貝 bars thin, incomplete, shifted right.

231 - Obv. field slightly smaller than in 228, rev. similar. QIAN head with nose near middle, slightly angled up; 日 bar short, slightly shifted left. ZHONG head relatively thin, evenly tapering. BAO cap irregular, with raised shoulders, 尔 not connecting to right side of cap; dots small, angled out; top bar of 王 tilted downward to right; 貝 bars shifted left; legs small, asymmetrical, left larger than right.

232 - Fields similar to 231. Characters thin. QIAN head small, with thin nose near middle, angled up; 日 bar short, shifted right. ZHONG head with detached tip; 田 with sharp spine on upper right corner. BAO with left side of cap extending into outer rim, which is trimmed away around it; 尔 with both dots small, angled out; 王 top bar reduced; 貝 bars connecting left; breaks in upper right side and near top left corner of 貝.

233 - Obv. field smaller than in 232, rev. similar. Characters very similar to 232, including BAO cap overlapping into outer rim and detached tip of ZHONG head. While 233 could be worn example of 232, some differences do not seem entirely attributable to wear; left leg of YUAN, for example, longer and more deeply curved than in 232, touching outer rim over broader distance.

234 - Fields slightly smaller than in 233. QIAN head small, with short nose near middle, angled up; bar in 日 long, incomplete, centered. ZHONG head long, thin, curved, uniform in thickness; 田 narrow, not close to outer rim. BAO with left dot in 尔 vertical, right dot angled, overlapping into inner rim; bars in 貝 appear to be connected left. Outer rim not cut away for left side of BAO cap as in preceding two vars.

235 - Fields similar to 231. Outer rims moderately wide, rev. inner rim narrow. QIAN with bar in 日 long, nearly complete, centered. ZHONG 田 nearly rectangular. Left dot in BAO 尔 appears to be vertical; bars in 貝 long, touching sides, centered. Characters in rubbed coin in low relief; raised line from casting crack crossing rims on reverse indicates faces were not ground and are not greatly worn.

236 - Similar to 232; characters thin; fields slightly smaller than in 232. QIAN as in 232, but bulb on 乙 larger; 十 with left side of horizontal stroke detached. YUAN with unusual, curled barb. ZHONG head markedly curved, with right end thick, bulbous; 田 wide, reaching inner and outer rims, nearly rectangular. BAO cap broken on top on left side (also in 237 and 238); 尔 dots small, left dot vertical; 貝 bars long, shifted left; break in top of 貝 near right corner, as occurs in var. 219 above. Wide rev. inner rim. Rubbed coin with hole weakly roseate. Vars. 236–238 are all similar to Yoshida's Y144, with 237 most similar to that var.

237 - Fields as in 236; rev. inner rim similarly wide. QIAN head small, with nose near base, angled up. Hook on main bar of YUAN swollen; right leg without curled barb. ZHONG head similar in shape to that in 236, but not as markedly bulbous on right; 田 more strongly tapering on both sides. BAO similar to 236, with break in top of 貝 near upper right corner, and vertical left dot in 尔.

238 - Fields as in 236; rev. inner rim similarly wide. QIAN with 日 bar short, centered; head with long nose near middle, angled up; 乙 shaft with small, circular bulb. YUAN left leg deeply recurved, broadly appressed to rim; right leg incised from rim. BAO with bars in 貝 centered; both dots in 尔 angled out. As in 236 and 237, break in top of 貝 near upper right corner. Hole taller than wide.

229	230	231	232	233	234
23.2 mm	23.7 mm	23.7 mm	22.5 mm	22.8 mm	22.7 mm
1	1	1	1	1	1
670	9B	9-cc3	9-O	679	678

235	236	237	238	239	
23.7 mm	22.8 mm	22.7 mm	22.5 mm	22.4 mm	
1	1	1 Y144	1	1	
859	322	1069	816	9F	

239 - Fields as in 236; characters tilted slightly to right. Rubbed coin unusually thin. QIAN head with short, horizontal nose in middle; bar in 日 long, nearly complete. YUAN left leg raised from rim. ZHONG head moderately bulbous on right side; 田 rectangular, wide, nearly reaching inner and outer rims. BAO 貝 bars appear to be shifted left; 尔 tiny, laterally compressed, dots indistinct.

Addendum to this group - See entry 455, p. 109.

See also var. 145, p. 51.

POWERFUL, STRONG (遒勁, *shû kei*)

The characters are wide and YUAN has a long, sharply bent left hook and short top bar. Yoshida lists one plain-reverse variety and two with reverse mark. Doo (2003: p. 95) illustrates two coins in this group (24.9–25.5 mm) and lists them as "Valued 10" but does not explain why he considers them as other than value-1.

240 - Bar in QIAN 日 long, centered or shifted right; complete or connected right in worn coins. ZHONG bar 1 complete, meeting inner and outer rims. Bars in BAO 貝 appear complete, but finely incised from sides in unworn coins; 貝 legs directed horizontally. Rev. inner rim moderately wide.

241 - Fields as in 240. Intentional break in upper left corner of QIAN 日. Left leg YUAN sharply bent in middle. BAO 貝 legs thin, angled down.

242 - Fields as in 240, but thin characters. ZHONG bar 1 short, incised from inner rim and not reaching outer rim. BAO with bars in 貝 long, centered, tapering; legs small.

STRONG YUAN (勁元, *kei gen*)

As in the previous group, the main bar of YUAN has a conspicuous, sharply bent left hook, but here the hook reaches the bottom left corner of the inner rim, and the top bar on YUAN is long. QIAN 乙 has a narrow, angular base. The central vertical stroke in BAO 尔 is disconnected, giving three dots. The BAO 貝 legs are short, stubby, and slightly asymmetrical, the left not meeting the outer rim and the right close to the inner rim. Yoshida lists one plain reverse variety and one with reverse mark.

243 - Most coins have same field sizes as rubbed coin, but about 20% have either obv. or rev. field slightly larger. Coins with markedly larger rev. field are 244. There is some variation, partly due to wear, in the size of the QIAN and ZHONG heads, thickness of the obverse inner rim, and size of the BAO 貝 legs.

244 - Obv. field similar to 243, rev. markedly larger.

245 - Fields as in 243. Obv. and rev. outer rims narrow; rev. inner rim wide. Characters thin, BAO 尔 tall, with long dots.

246 - Similar to 245; but flan thin; rev. inner rim quite narrow. BAO small; 尔 small; bars in 貝 shifted right.

240	241	242			
24.1–25.0 mm	24.6 mm	25.0 mm			

9	Y207	1		1						

883   884   886

243	244	245	246		
23.2–24.5 mm	24.0–25.0 mm	22.5 mm	22.8 mm		

141	Y210U	44		1		1				

767-r2   1072   2A   65

DEFECTIVE HEAD ZHONG (短頭重, *tan tô chô*)

The ZHONG head is small and defective. These coins are similar to the Large Characters group above, with ZHONG 田 narrower than in the Wide Characters group, and closer to the inner than the outer rim. The right leg of YUAN is shallowly curved, usually with a narrow base. The cap of BAO is asymmetrical, with the right shoulder having a sharper angle than the left. Yoshida numbers two plain reverse varieties. None of the coins shown here is unambiguously identifiable with any of Yoshida's four illustrations.

247 - QIAN head straight, perpendicular to 日, nose below middle, slightly angled up; bar in 日 long, shifted left. YUAN with long, shallowly curved left leg; right leg evenly curved, reaching outer rim, incised from rim in unworn coins. YUAN top bar unusually short. BAO with 貝 bars centered; legs small, thin, asymmetrical, neither leg meeting adjacent border. Rev. outer rim wide.

248 - Similar to 247, but flan and obv. field smaller. QIAN head tall, not perpendicular; bar in 日 nearly complete; 乙 shaft lacking bulb. Top bar on YUAN longer than in 247. Dot between left and right parts of QIAN may be casting error. BAO cap with head offset to left.

249 - Field sizes as in 248. QIAN, BAO bars incomplete, centered. QIAN with small, short head not reaching outer rim; right side of 十 longer than left; shaft of 乙 slightly hooked at top, lacking bulb, barb relatively small.

250 - Obv. field slightly smaller than in 248, rev. field appears to be larger (?). Characters tilted to right. QIAN 日 with complete bar, 乙 shaft with large bulb. Right leg YUAN with base broadly appressed to outer rim. ZHONG 田 square on left side, tapering on right. BAO 貝 with bars shifted right; left leg thin, meeting outer rim; right leg thicker, not meeting inner rim.

251 - Fields slightly smaller than in 248. QIAN head tilted to right; 乙 shaft with bulb. ZHONG 田 rectangular; bar 2 meeting inner rim.

252 - Obv. field slightly smaller than in 248; rev. inner rim moderately wide. QIAN head only slightly curved, nearly perpendicular; 日 with long bar shifted left; 乙 shaft with bulb. Right leg YUAN broadly contacting outer rim. BAO 貝 with very short bars, shifted slightly to right; legs thick.

253 - Obv. field as in 248, rev. smaller. Characters similar to 252, but bar in QIAN 日 complete or nearly so. YUAN right leg meeting outer rim at turn of barb; barb sharp. BAO right leg long, thin, meeting inner rim, left leg truncate, not meeting outer rim.

254 - Fields large, obv. as in 247, rev. larger. Obv. outer rim moderately narrow. QIAN 十 with right side of horizontal stroke detached; top of 乙 with only slight bulb, merging with outer rim. YUAN right leg with barb blunt. BAO 王 and 尔 distinct; 尔 dots independent, teardrop shaped; 貝 legs bulbous, directed horizontally, right larger than left, neither reaching adjacent rim.

255 - Fields similar to 248. QIAN with tall, slightly curved head, nose small, below middle; 乙 shaft with large, irregularly circular bulb; barb blunt. YUAN main bar slightly tilted down to left; right leg with heavy, triangular barb. ZHONG 田 close to inner rim. BAO 貝 legs thin, symmetrical, angled down. Rev. inner rim quite wide.

256 - Field sizes similar to 254, obv. outer rim narrower. Characters similar, but QIAN head straighter; 乙 bulb large. YUAN right leg with small, sharp barb. ZHONG head quite reduced, circular. BAO 尔 dots fused with horizontal stroke. BAO 貝 with left leg thicker than right.

247	248	249	250	251	252
25.2–25.5 mm	23.7 mm	22.8 mm	23.0 mm	23.3 mm	23.3 mm
2	1	1	1	1	1

1030	53	606	974	284	498

253	254	255	256	257	258
22.8 mm	23.4 mm	23.3 mm	23.3 mm	22.5 mm	22.7 mm
1	1	1	1	1	1

1051	586	898	922	467	68

257 - Obv. field as in 254 and 256; rev. smaller; obv. outer rim thin. QIAN head tall, short nose below middle; bar in 日 appears complete. ZHONG 田 tapering on both sides. BAO with narrow, laterally compressed 王; 貝 legs thin, symmetrical.

258 - Fields as in 254. Obv. outer rim thin. Characters small, thin. QIAN with tall, thin, slightly curved head, thin nose below middle; 乙 shaft with bulb, separate from outer rim; bar in 日 thin, complete. YUAN right leg incised from outer rim. BAO with 王 quite laterally compressed; 尔 small, with tiny, linear dots; 貝 bars centered; legs quite small, nearly symmetrical.

259 - Fields as in 254. Obv. outer rim thin. QIAN head perpendicular, nose below middle; 日 with incomplete bar shifted left. YUAN right leg shallowly curved. BAO 貝 bars shifted right; legs markedly larger than in 258.

259
22.8 mm
1

467A

SHAGGY CHARACTERS (尨字, *bô ji*)

QIAN 日 and ZHONG 田 are wide, vertically compressed. The left leg of YUAN is nearly straight; the right leg is sharply bent, incised from the outer rim. The BAO cap is shallow and asymmetrical. Yoshida lists two plain-reverse varieties.

260 - Fits the description above. Other variety illustrated by Yoshida (Y217) has wider head on BAO cap and ZHONG head is thin. In rubbed coin, middle horizontal stroke in ZHONG 田 scarcely evident and not showing in rubbing.

SWOLLEN CHARACTERS (肥字, *hi ji*)

ZHONG and BAO are more or less centered between the inner and outer rims. ZHONG is relaxed rather than compact. The left leg of YUAN is short and sharply bent toward the end; the right leg has a blunt barb. The BAO cap is tall, with long sides, and nearly symmetrical; the head is unusually small; the 貝 legs are small, more or less horizontally directed, and usually do not meet the adjacent rims. Yoshida lists six varieties, all with plain reverse. All four coins used for rubbings here have the obverse side with parts of characters obscured, due to a combination of poor casting and wear. None of these four coins is unambiguously identifiable with any of Yoshida's illustrations for this group.

261 - QIAN head slightly back-curved, with long nose in middle; 日 wide, with long bar shifted left; 十 irregular, horizontal stroke tilted down to left; base of 乙 forming obtuse angle with shaft and extending past right side of inner rim. YUAN left leg raised from outer rim, sharply bent; right leg incised or raised from rim. ZHONG 田 rectangular. BAO 貝 legs asymmetrical, right leg thicker, angled down, extending below level of inner rim, neither leg touching adjacent rim.

262 - Fields similar to 261. QIAN head strongly back-curved, with nose at base; 日 with bar short, centered; 十 incised from inner rim, horizontal stroke not tilted; base of 乙 forming less than right angle with shaft and extending markedly past right side of inner rim. YUAN left leg shorter than in 261; neither leg reaching adjacent rim. ZHONG 田 slightly tapering on right side.

263 - Fields similar to 261. QIAN head with long, horizontal nose below middle; 日 with complete bar; 乙 base at nearly right angle to shaft, base swollen at end but without barb, extending past right side of inner rim. YUAN left leg not sharply bent. ZHONG with both sides of 田 tapering. BAO legs thin, asymmetrical, left longer than right, neither touching adjacent rim.

264 - Slightly smaller obv. field and markedly smaller rev. field than in 261. QIAN with short head not touching outer rim, nose below middle, angled up; 日 with complete bar; 乙 with narrow base, scarcely extending past right side of inner rim. YUAN with sharply bent left leg. BAO narrow. Rubbed coin quite worn on obverse.

260					
24.3 mm					
1	Y216					

876

261	262	263	264		
24.5 mm	24.3 mm	23.7 mm	23.8 mm		
1	1	1	1		

240 908 1057 924

TOWERING YUAN (聳元, *shô gen*)

This is one of the most common types of QYZB; var. 265 is the single most abundant variety among the coins examined for this guide. The group is distinctive. QIAN has a conspicuous, back-curved head; the bar in 日 is short, centered; the base of 乙 is right-angled, wide, and straight. YUAN is tall, with a short top bar and with the left leg not deeply curved. BAO 王 and 尔 are unusually small; 尔 is m-shaped, and 王 is well separated from the cap of BAO on the left side, perhaps the easiest feature to look for. Here three different ranges of flan size are distinguished: SMALL, 21.4–22.8 mm, with larger (e.g. 271) or smaller (e.g. 272) reverse fields; MEDIUM, 22.9–23.7 mm (e.g. 265); and LARGE (uncommon), larger than 24 mm (e.g. 277). Within these classes, varieties can differ in field sizes. The range of flan and field sizes in this series suggests that multiple different models were involved in production, though it is challenging to delineate discrete varieties within what amounts to nearly continuous size variation. There is subtle variation in details of the characters as well (e.g., shape and size of bulb on 乙 shaft; width of bases of 乙 and YUAN right leg; shape and size of BAO 王; and possibly character size), but more study is needed to determine whether consistent varieties can be delineated based on this variation. A complicating factor, as in other groups, is wear. The wear example (p. 19) in the introductory material shows the significant effects of wear on the characters in var. 457 (Addendum). Yoshida numbers two varieties in this group based on outer-rim widths, both with plain reverse: Y231 (23.5 mm; wider rims) and Y232 (22.5 mm; narrower rims). These represent the medium and small categories here, but his entries have similar field sizes, except for the reverse field in Y232L.

265 - Most common variety. Medium-sized flan. Rev. inner rim usually narrow to moderately narrow; about 3% of coins have wider rev. inner rim than typical but are not classified as separate variety here. Diameter of rubbed coin 23.7 mm, at large end of size range; smaller coins have correspondingly narrower outer rims.

266 - Like 265, medium flan, but smaller reverse field, as in 272 below.

267 - Like 265, but break in upper left corner of BAO 貝.

268 - Obv. and rev. fields both larger than in 265. Rev. inner rim narrow in about half the coins, somewhat wider in rest.

269 - Field sizes as in 268 (larger than in 265), but flan small, obv. and rev. outer rims narrow; rev. inner rim narrow.

270 - Rev. field as in 265, obv. field larger. Characters thin. Right leg of YUAN with base narrower than usual, incised from outer rim.

271 - Small flan. Field sizes as in 265, outer rims narrower. Rev. inner rim narrow or somewhat wider.

272 - Small flan, nearly same size range as in 271. Obv. field as in 265, rev. field smaller.

273 - Red copper rather than bronze. Fields similar to 272; rev. inner rim moderately wide. Small hole. Characters thick, crudely cast. QIAN head with nose lacking; oblong bulb on shaft of 乙. BAO with narrow 王, shaped like comma in rubbed coin, wider but narrower than normal in other; 貝 legs thick.

274 - Red copper rather than bronze. Field sizes as in 272; rev. outer rim moderately wide. BAO smaller than in 272, 273; 王 relatively wide.

275 - Large flan, fields, and characters. Fields larger than in 268. QIAN head unusual in shape; flat on top, nose merged with back-curved head.

265	266	267	268	269	270
22.9–23.7 mm	23.5–23.6 mm	23.3 mm	23.3–24.0 mm	21.8–22.4 mm	23.7 mm
305	Y231	3	1	25	3	4

994	762	763	3a-2	764	903

271	272	273	274	275	276
21.4–22.8 mm	21.6–22.7 mm	22.5–22.7 mm	23.0 mm	24.4 mm	24.2 mm
93	40	2	1	1	1

3-m2	3B	674	553	3E	675

276 - Large flan; obv. field as in 275, rev field larger. QIAN head large; YUAN tall; ZHONG head thin, evenly curved. Coin thin; characters in low relief. Rev. inner rim narrow.

277 - Large flan; fields similar to 276. Characters thin; similar to those in 276 but bases of QIAN 乙 and YUAN right leg narrower, ZHONG head thicker, BAO smaller.

278 - Flan and fields oblong; hole taller than wide.

Addendum to this group - See entry 457, p. 109.

277	278
24.2 x 24.8	22.5 x 24.1 mm
1	1

761	677

WIDE HOLE (廣穿, *kô sen*)

The hole is proportionally larger than usual for QYZB. QIAN 乙 is roughly L-shaped, with a straight, wide base; the bulb on the shaft has a distinct hook. The bars in QIAN 日 and BAO 貝 are invariably incomplete, centered. YUAN has the hook on the main bar angled toward the right leg of BAO; the YUAN left leg is long and shallowly curved; the right leg is raised from the outer rim and has a conspicuous barb, usually angled back. ZHONG is relaxed rather than compact. Yoshida illustrates two standard-sized coins of this type, as well as two different small-flan coins under Y234. Although most coins having fields as in 279 will be that common variety, some other varieties have the same field sizes. 286 and 287 differ from other vars in having the main bar of YUAN truncated, and from one another in the size of the characters.

279 - Obv. and rev. outer rims moderately wide. QIAN nose originating at lower 1/3 of head, angled slightly upward. ZHONG head thick. Rev. inner rim variable, narrow or wider, but not markedly wide. Break in top of BAO cap near right corner occurs fairly commonly.

280 - Like 279, but characters thin; QIAN head smaller.

281 - Similar to 280, with thin characters, but larger flan and fields; left leg of YUAN longer.

282 - Obv. field as in 281, rev. larger. Characters and obv. inner rim thin. YUAN tall, with long left leg; right leg small, raised, and more tightly curled than in 281. ZHONG head smaller than in 281.

283 - Like 279, but central vertical stroke in ZHONG continued below base.

284 - Fields as in 279; characters similar, but QIAN head with nose at base, angled up. YUAN with short top bar and shallowly curved left leg meeting outer rim at high angle.

285 - Like 279, but rev. field slightly smaller. Irregular dot in obv. lower left quadrant. QIAN head with very thin nose. YUAN left leg with sharp bend. ZHONG small.

286 - Like 279 but YUAN with truncated main bar, short top bar. Obv. inner rim wide.

287 - Like 286, with truncated main bar of YUAN, but smaller, thinner characters; obv. inner rim thin. QIAN head smaller, with nose near base. Top bar YUAN longer. ZHONG with longer base, thinner head.

288 - Asymmetrical, taller than wide. Obv. field somewhat larger than in 279, rev. field markedly larger. Characters large. Rubbed coin shows roseate hole.

289 - Fields slightly to markedly smaller than in 279; rev. outer and inner rims wide. QIAN head with nose near base, slightly angled up.

290 - Similar to 289, but slightly smaller flan, characters, fields; coin thin. Right side of ZHONG 田 taller than left. Rev. inner rim narrower than in 289.

291 - Obv. field slightly smaller than in 279, rev. field markedly smaller. Coin crude, poorly cast. Zhong head reduced, bulbous. Rev. inner rim moderately wide.

292 - Small flan, characters; fields similar to 290. Characters tilted slightly to right. Rubbed coin roughly cast and unfinished; edges have not been filed and casting sprue remains. YUAN left leg short, raised from outer rim. Rev. inner rim narrow. Recorded as excavated from Shanxi Province.

279	280	281	282	283	284
23.5–24.6 mm	23.5–24.0 mm	24.5–24.7 mm	24.6 mm	24.2 mm	24.2 mm
205	Y233	10		2		1		1		1	

285	286	287	288	289	290
24.0 mm	24.5 mm	24.2 mm	25.3 x 24.6 mm	23.5–24.0 mm	22.7–23.3 mm
1		1		1		1		3		2	Y234U

291	292
22.8 mm	22.3 mm
1		1	

293 - Fields as in 290; characters smaller. Obv. inner rim quite thin. Coin with high copper content.

294 - Small flan; characters similar in size to 293; fields somewhat smaller than in 293; obv. outer rim narrow; obv. inner rim thin.

WIDE HOLE, THIN CHARACTERS (廣穿細字, *kô sen sai ji*)

This group is similar to the preceding group, but the flan and characters are typically smaller. As in the Wide Hole group, the hole is proportionally large. QIAN 乙 has a similarly long, flat base, but the bulb on the shaft is evenly rounded rather than forming a hook. The right leg of YUAN is not raised from the outer rim, but typically contacts it at the turn of the barb. As in the Wide Hole group, ZHONG is relaxed rather than compact. Yoshida numbers two types, both plain reverse, differing in flan size. One comprises larger coins (22.3–22.7 mm), with Yoshida's two examples differing in rev. field size; the other comprises smaller coins (19.1–21.2 mm), with the two examples differing in the sizes of both fields.

295 - Moderately broad outer rims; coins with larger flan tend to have wider outer rims. Rev. inner rim variable but moderate, neither very thin nor very wide. Right leg of 元 usually with pronounced barb.

296 - Like 295, but ZHONG with break in top of 田 near left corner; ZHONG base not reaching inner rim; BAO with taller 王 and 尔; right dot missing in 尔.

297 - Obv. field slightly smaller than in 295; rev. with presumed nail mark and dot. The nail mark is not in a typical position for a reverse mark, and the dot may be a casting defect.

298 - Obv. field as in 295 or slightly larger, rev. field consistently larger. Outer rims tend to be slightly narrower than in 295.

WIDE HOLE, SWOLLEN CHARACTERS (廣穿肥字, *kô sen hi ji*)

This group is similar to the preceding two groups, with a proportionally large hole and relaxed ZHONG. YUAN is short, with a strong, nearly vertical hook on the main bar; the left leg is strongly curved, often slightly recurved, and the right leg broadly meets the outer rim. The bars in BAO 目 are short, incomplete, and usually shifted to the right. There is variation in this group in flan size, character size, outer rim widths, and rev. inner rim width. As with the Towering Yuan group above, there is subtle variation in features of the characters, but more study is needed to determine whether it is possible to delineate consistent varieties based on this variation. Vars 300 and 301 have somewhat larger fields than the other coins in the group. Common vars 299 and 303 have similar obv. fields, but the reverse is smaller in 303; intermediates occur, but most coins fall into one variety or the other. Yoshida numbers three types, all plain reverse; two of them respectively represent larger- and smaller-flan coins; the third (which is rare) has small fields, very wide outer rims, and thick characters.

299 - Obv. and rev. outer rims moderately wide; varying in width with flan size. Rev. inner rim ranging from moderately narrow, as in rubbing 299, to somewhat wider, as seen in rubbing 303 #1.

293	294		295		296		297		298	
21.8 mm	20.2 mm		22.6–24.2 mm		22.7 mm		22.6 mm		22.7–23.4 mm	
1	1	Y234L	48	Y235L	1		1		27	Y235U
1084	504		4		997		4G		4a-r2	

299		300	301	302	303 #1	303 #2
22.8–23.7 mm		23.3 mm	23.9 mm	24.0 mm	22.2–23.7 mm	
186	Y237	1	1	2	151	
1		1075	765	1-c	1076	1-d

300 - Characters thin. Obv. field similar to 299; rev. field somewhat larger; rev. inner rim quite narrow.

301 - Obv. field somewhat larger than in 300, rev. field similar to 300. Characters thin and very similar to those in 300, but legs of YUAN incised from outer rim. Rev. inner rim relatively wide.

302 - Fields similar to 299. Wide obv. and rev. outer rims. Characters large, thick.

303 - Obv. field similar to 299 or slightly smaller; rev. field distinctly smaller. Rev. inner rim moderately wide (303 #1). About 20% of coins have a somewhat wider rev. inner rim (303 #2) but are not here classed as a separate variety.

304 - Small flan; fields slightly smaller than in 303 but characters similar in size. Bars in BAO 貝 distinctive; short, triangular, shifted far right.

305 - Fields similar to 303, but characters smaller. QIAN head and BAO 王 and 尔 are small. Left leg YUAN short, contacting outer rim at end, not recurved.

306 - Small flan; fields, characters similar to 305; differs from 305 in having left leg YUAN longer, recurved.

307 - Fields smaller than in 303; QIAN and YUAN smaller than in preceding two vars. Hole unusually large, with very thin but distinct obv. inner rim, close to ZHONG 田 and BAO 目.

308 - Fields similar to 307. Characters larger than in 307, similar in size to those in 305. Coin crudely cast; characters shallow and vague, even though rubbed coin not appreciably worn; both obv. and rev. slipped (offset from center of flan). ZHONG 田 and BAO 目 nearly touching inner rim. Coin not finished; edge rough, only some high spots filed.

SWOLLEN CHARACTERS, SEPARATED FROM OUTER RIM
(肥字刔輪, *hi ji ketsu rin*)

Similar to the preceding group, but QIAN and YUAN are clearly separated from the outer rim. YUAN has an irregular appearance; both legs are deeply curved, and the right leg has a conspicuous barb; the hook on the main bar is angled toward BAO rather than vertical.

309 - Obv. outer rim relatively narrow. QIAN and YUAN not touching outer rim; ZHONG 田 and BAO 目 closer to inner than to outer rim. BAO with 目 asymmetrical, higher on right than on left; BAO legs thin. In some coins, BAO shows break in right side of cap; in 尔, dots, vertical stroke, and part of cap are fused, forming asterisk-like shape. Coins with thin characters may have dots distinct, as in Yoshida's Y240U. All four coins examined show obv. inner rim with small, acute spine on three corners (upper left and right, lower left).

WIDE YI (濶乙, *katsu otsu*)

The characters are somewhat irregular. QIAN has the 乙 base nearly as wide as the shaft is tall, with a slight barb. YUAN has a short top bar; the right leg is shallowly curved and incised from the outer rim. ZHONG has a small, thick head and 田 is vertically compressed. BAO 王 and 尔 are small, with 尔 m-shaped and free from the cap; the 貝 legs are small. Yoshida numbers two plain-reverse varieties and two with rev. mark.

310 - Larger flan, fitting the description above. Outer rims moderately wide.

311 - Smaller flan, fitting the description above. ZHONG and BAO well spaced from outer rim.

304	305	306	307	308	
21.7 x 22.3 mm	21.9 mm	22.2 mm	21.6 mm	22.2 mm	
1	1	1	1	1	
1002	900	1a	359	1-f	
309		**310**	**311**		
21.7–22.0 mm		23.3–24.0 mm	22.5 mm		
4	Y240L	2	Y243	1	Y244		

309		310	311		
21.7–22.0 mm		23.3–24.0 mm	22.5 mm		
4	Y240L	2	Y243	1	Y244		
1-b		1007	880		

SLANTING YUAN (俯元, *fu gen*)

QIAN is tall; 乙 has a relatively narrow base and often only a slight barb, producing a shallow hook. YUAN is wider than tall; the left leg is short and slightly curved; the right leg is long and gradually curved, often with the barb small. The main bar of YUAN has a weak left hook and is sometimes tilted slightly down to the left, which is the origin of Yoshida's name for this group. ZHONG is usually relaxed or semi-relaxed rather than compact, the head is usually long and narrow, and 田 often has the center horizontal stroke weak or incomplete, not reaching the sides. BAO has a wide, more or less symmetrical cap; the head is typically small. The BAO legs are variable, directed horizontally, or curved or angled downward, but usually small. In larger coins, BAO 王 is usually ladderlike, with horizontal strokes of roughly equal length. In coins smaller than 23 mm, 王 is often narrow, in some cases only an irregular squiggle. The dots in 尔 are usually distinct. Some reverse-mark coins in this group have the mark so faint they may be mistaken for plain-reverse coins, and in fact some of those could be included here. This is a diverse group. Yoshida numbers 43 varieties, of which 25 are plain reverse; 53 varieties are listed here. Doo (2003, p. 97) illustrates seven coins in this group (25.4–26.7 mm) and indicates them as being "Valued 10," but does not explain why he considers them as other than value-1.

312 - QIAN head back-curved, with long, horizontal nose near middle; 乙 with broad base, extending past edge of inner rim; base of 十 reaching inner rim but in rubbings appears separated because surface level lower than inner rim. Right leg of YUAN deeply bent, with long base incised from outer rim. ZHONG head long, narrow; 田 relatively short, wide, tapering more on right than on left; base long. Middle horizontal stroke in ZHONG 田 looks incomplete in rubbing, due to having low relief, but in coin is complete on both sides. BAO 貝 legs small, nearly symmetrical; 尔 with long vertical stroke and small dots. Rev. inner rim narrow.

313 - Fields slightly smaller than in 312. QIAN head small, straight, with short nose near middle, slightly angled up; 日 narrow, with short, centered bar; 十 horizontal stroke close to 日, bottom of 十 tapering, just touching inner rim; 乙 with narrower base than in 312. YUAN right leg shallowly curved, reaching outer rim in middle of base. ZHONG head long, thick; 田 more symmetrically tapering than in 312. BAO 貝 legs splayed, nearly horizontal, left nearly reaching outer rim; right not reaching inner rim. 313 and 314 are identical in field sizes and have characters similar to Yoshida's Y256. Y256 is named "severed inner rim," and both of Yoshida's examples have large break in top of obv. inner rim; hence neither 313 or 314 is equivalent to Y256.

314 - Fields as in 313; characters similar. QIAN 十 with horizontal stroke not tapering at bottom but incised from inner rim; 乙 with acute barb longer than in 313, but not showing in rubbing due to low relief. YUAN right leg more deeply curved, not touching outer rim. ZHONG head thinner; base shorter, well spaced from both inner and outer rims. BAO 貝 legs similar to 313.

315 - Obv. field similar to 313, rev. smaller. QIAN head straight, with short nose below middle; 日 bar incomplete, shifted left; base of 乙 narrow. ZHONG with small, horizontal head; 田 deeper than in 314, asymmetrical, tapering more on right side than on left; central horizontal stroke tapering at each end, sometimes incomplete; ZHONG base not reaching inner rim. BAO 尔 with horizontal stroke free from cap in less-worn coins; 貝 legs splayed, directed almost horizontally; in less-worn coins, left leg reaching outer rim, right leg not reaching inner rim.

316 - Fields similar to 313. Characters similar to 315, but thinner; rev. inner rim narrow. Top of BAO cap wider. YUAN main bar tilted down to left.

312	313	314	315	316	317
25.6 mm	25.6 mm	25.0 mm	24.1–25.5 mm	25.5 mm	25.4 mm
1 Y250	1 cf. Y256U	1 cf. Y256L	8 Y257	1	1

799	1043	1022	907	136	584

318	319
26.2 mm	23.4 mm
1 cf. Y258	1

789	137

317 - Fields similar to 312. Narrow outer rims. QIAN head straight; 乙 with relatively wide base. YUAN right leg deeply curved, base narrow. ZHONG base narrow, not touching inner or outer rims. BAO 貝 narrow; legs thin, left slightly lower than right. Rev. inner rim narrow.

318 - Fields similar to 313. QIAN with tall, back-curved head; base of 乙 unusually small. ZHONG 田 with middle horizontal stroke incomplete; ZHONG base long, reaching outer rim, incised from inner rim. BAO legs thick, angled down at 45 degrees, reaching slightly lower than bottom of inner rim. Obv. inner rim thin. Similar to Yoshida's Y258 but has somewhat larger fields, slightly larger characters, taller QIAN, wider YUAN, longer left leg of BAO 貝.

319 - Similar to 318 in tiny base of QIAN 乙 and shape of BAO legs, but flan, fields, and characters smaller. Obv. inner and outer rims narrow. QIAN head small, straight, with nose below middle, angled up; bar in 日 short, centered. YUAN right leg deeply bent, base short. ZHONG head thin; 田 wide, with incomplete middle horizontal stroke. BAO legs asymmetrical, left thicker, just touching outer rim, right thinner, not meeting inner rim. Rev. inner rim moderately wide. Apparent obv. dot to right of YUAN may be casting error, as it is the tip of larger casting defect nearly impinging on YUAN right leg.

320 - Fields similar to or slightly smaller than in 313. QIAN 十 incised from inner rim; bar in 日 incomplete, centered; 乙 base narrow, sloping down. ZHONG 田 wide, deep, strongly tapering on both sides, middle horizontal stroke incomplete; base wide, reaching outer rim, incised from inner. BAO with 王 narrow; 尔 dots distinct; 貝 with incomplete bars; legs thin, straight, angled down; left leg longer, reaching outer rim, right not reaching inner rim. This is Yoshida's Y267 and/or Y268, which seem to grade into one another.

321 - Fields similar to 320. Characters similar, but thicker, more robust. YUAN left leg longer and right leg shorter. ZHONG 田 nearly rectangular, square on right, slightly tapering on left. BAO 王 and 尔 larger, heavier; right dot in 尔 oval rather than linear. Rubbed coin has raised, angular mark on rev. that may be casting artifact.

322 - Fields similar to 320. Characters thin. QIAN head small, straight, nose in middle, slightly angled up; 日 bar nearly complete; 乙 base shallow, evenly curved. ZHONG head thin, horizontal. BAO 尔 with horizontal stroke slanting up to right; 貝 bars incomplete, shifted left; legs small, widely spaced, nearly symmetrical, left tiny, right longer. Similar to 327 and 339 below.

323 - Fields similar to 320. QIAN 十 short, bottom widely separated from inner rim; 乙 with wide, strong base. ZHONG 田 with break in upper left corner; middle horizontal stroke incomplete; base short, not meeting either rim. YUAN with long left leg. BAO 王 ladderlike; 貝 legs somewhat angular; asymmetrical, left larger, blunt, reaching outer rim; right thin, acute, not reaching inner rim.

324 - Fields larger than in 320. QIAN 乙 with small base; 日 bar shifted right. ZHONG head long, horizontal. YUAN right leg with only slight barb. BAO legs nearly symmetrical, left leg slightly thicker and touching outer rim, right leg incised from inner rim.

325 - Obv. field smaller than in 320, rev. similar. QIAN head short, nose sandwiched between 日 and outer rim; 日 rectangular, with thick outline and very thin, complete bar in reduced space; QIAN 十 reaching inner rim. ZHONG head relatively large, close to outer rim. BAO 貝 with thick outline; bars thin, irregular in reduced space.

326 - Fields similar to 320. QIAN head very slightly curved; 日 tapering, bar centered; 乙 with relatively wide base. YUAN short; right leg short, with small barb. ZHONG head large; 田 strongly tapering on both sides as in 320, 324, 325; BAO legs asymmetrical; left leg thick, reaching outer rim; right leg smaller, thinner, angled down toward hook of YUAN. Rev. inner rim wide.

327 - Fields somewhat smaller than in 320. Characters thin. QIAN head only slightly curved, nose close to base, angled up; bar in QIAN 日 thin, complete. YUAN left leg short, shallowly curved; right leg reaching outer rim at turn of barb; barb small, thin. ZHONG head small. BAO small; cap symmetrical, sides short, left side incised from outer rim; 王 narrow, horizontal strokes often thin; 尔 often weakly connected to cap on top and right side; dots small; bars in 貝 long, nearly complete; legs small, asymmetrical; left curved, right straighter, one or other sometimes reaching adjacent rim. Four coins have nose on QIAN head arising closer to base than shown in rubbing, and more strongly angled up. Characters somewhat similar to Yoshida's Y277, with identical field sizes, but that var. has crescent below hole on rev. Compare with 322 above and 339 below.

328 - Fields somewhat smaller than in 327; characters small; weakly cast, in low relief; outer rims and rev. inner rim moderately wide. QIAN 乙 with base at obtuse angle to shaft, barb scarcely evident. ZHONG short, more vertically compressed than usual, with thin head. BAO legs tiny, nearly symmetrical.

329 - Fields small, similar to 328. Characters larger than in 328, similar to 327 but thicker.

330 - Fields and characters similar to 327; flan smaller, outer rims narrower. YUAN right leg more

320	321	322	323	324	325
25.0–25.2 mm	25.2 mm	25.0 mm	25.2 mm	25.5 mm	24.2 mm
4 Y267/268	1	1	1 cf Y269	1	1

251	795	1004	772	146	245

326	327	328	329	330	331
25.2 mm	23.5–24.4 mm	24.0 mm	22.8 mm	23.5 mm	23.5 mm
1	10 cf. Y277	1 Y273	1 Y275	1	1

773	776	32A	779	1015	49

deeply curved than in 327. ZHONG head larger. BAO cap deeper, asymmetrical, left side longer and at different angle than right.

331 - Fields as in 328. Characters similar to 329, but smaller; QIAN head shorter, back-curved, nose near base, angled up; YUAN right leg with deeper bend.

332 - Small flan; obv. field similar to 327, rev. somewhat smaller. Coins roughly cast. Obv. outer rim narrow. Although characters somewhat similar to 327, 332 was cast in smaller flan size (remnants of casting sprues evident), rather than being edge filed to small size.

333 - Obv. field as in 328, rev. slightly larger. QIAN head with nose at base, angled up; 日 tapering on both sides; 十 asymmetrical. Top bar of YUAN unusually long. ZHONG head long, thin; 田 tapering more on left than on right.

332	333
21.8–22.8 mm	23.1 mm
3	1

1091	973

334 - Coin asymmetrical. Minimum obv. field diameter as in 328, rev. slightly larger. QIAN head short, with long nose near base, angled up; 十 incised from inner rim. ZHONG 田 with small break in top near upper right corner; middle horizontal stroke incomplete on both sides. YUAN with right leg evenly curved, thick. BAO with vertical stroke in 尔 tilted, hooked to left; BAO legs asymmetrical, angular; left leg relatively large, reaching outer rim; right leg tiny. Rev. inner rim moderately wide.

335 - Obv. field as in 328; rev. smaller. All rims moderately wide. QIAN head back-curved, nose curved up; 乙 with wide base, swollen barb extending past side of inner rim. YUAN right leg with broad base. ZHONG 田 deep, touching inner rim. BAO 貝 legs similar to 334 but thicker.

336 - Coin asymmetrical; minimum obv. field diameter larger than in 328, minimum rev. diameter similar. QIAN head erect, slightly curved; nose short, horizontal; 日 bar short, centered; base of 乙 narrow. ZHONG 田 rectangular. Rev. inner rim moderately wide.

337 - Fields as in 328. Outer rims and rev. inner rim wide. QIAN head small, with horizontal nose near base; 日 bar long, shifted left; 乙 base shallow, with slight barb. ZHONG head thick; 田 tapering more on right than on left. BAO legs small, symmetrical, angled down.

338 - Fields slightly larger than in 328. Coin crudely cast, faces not finished. QIAN head small, straight, with horizontal nose in middle; 日 deep, scarcely tapering. ZHONG head thick; 田 strongly tapering on both sides. Head on BAO cap markedly off center to left.

Next 13 vars (339–351) mostly small coins (except for 339, diameter 23 mm or less) with BAO tall, relatively narrow, and having right leg directed down toward YUAN, reaching below level of inner rim; in all but 349, BAO tilted to right. Another useful feature is whether horizontal stroke in QIAN 十 is in middle (e.g. 340–342), or above middle, closer to 日 (e.g. 344, 345). This series similar to Yoshida's Y285, but none of entries here matches field sizes in Yoshida's rubbings.

339 - Fields similar to 338; characters thin. Bars in QIAN 日 and BAO 貝 thin, complete. QIAN head straight, with nose near middle, slightly angled up. ZHONG head small, thin; 田 nearly rectangular. BAO cap with left side shorter than right and incised from outer rim; head tiny; 貝 legs small, symmetrical, reaching lower than bottom of inner rim. Hole slightly broader than tall.

340 - Fields markedly smaller than in 339; outer rims and rev. inner rim wide. QIAN with short, straight head, short nose in middle; 日 nearly rectangular, with bar complete or nearly so; 乙 with barb slight. BAO 王 narrow; top of 尔 separate from cap, dots small; bars in 貝 long, nearly complete; legs asymmetrical, left leg nearly reaching outer rim. Similar to Yoshida's Y286, but that var. has rev. mark.

341 - Fields, characters similar to 340; smaller flan, outer rims and rev. inner rim narrower. Bars in BAO 貝 shorter. One coin retains part of casting sprue, indicating 341 was cast smaller than 340. 341 is similar to Yoshida's Y285 but differs in having taller QIAN, right side of ZHONG 田 more strongly tapering than left, and narrower reverse inner rim.

342 - Obv. field as in 340, rev. markedly smaller; characters thin, coin roughly cast. QIAN head small, straight, with short nose in middle; 日 bar complete. BAO with bars in 貝 long, incomplete. Obv. outer rim moderately narrow; rev. outer rim wide, rev. inner rim moderately wide.

343 - Obv. field somewhat smaller than in 340, rev. field markedly smaller, obv. outer rim narrower, rev. inner rim wide. ZHONG bar 2 longer on right than on left. BAO 貝 bars incomplete, irregular.

344 - Obv. field larger than in 340, rev. similar to 340; obv. outer rim narrow. QIAN head short, with long nose in middle; 乙 with strong barb. ZHONG with wide base. Bars in QIAN 日, BAO 貝 complete.

334	335	336	337	338	339
23.8 x 24.1 mm	24.3 mm	24.4 x 25.0 mm	24.5 mm	23.8 mm	24.1 mm
1	1	1	1	1	1

622, 774, 775, 32, 806, 469

340	341	342	343	344	345
23.0 mm	21.8–22.2 mm	21.5 mm	22.5 mm	21.5 mm	22.3 mm
2 cf. Y286	2 cf. Y285	1	1	1	1

259A, 926, 781, 208, 783, 1062

345 - Obv. markedly larger than in 340, rev. similar; obv. outer rim narrow. Characters thin, coin poorly cast, with parts of characters filled in with excess metal. QIAN tall; head with horizontal nose near middle; bar in 日 complete; 乙 with relatively long barb. YUAN tall, wide; main bar slightly tilted down to left. ZHONG head thin; 田 tapering. BAO 貝 legs small, symmetrical.

346 - Fields similar to 345. QIAN head short, with long nose, 日 relatively large. ZHONG 田 rectangular. BAO 貝 legs longer, thicker than in 345, nearly symmetrical.

347 - Obv. field similar to 340, rev. smaller; obv. outer rim narrow; rev. inner rim wide. Coin roughly cast. Characters small. QIAN head small, nose near middle, angled up. YUAN relatively tall, narrow. ZHONG 田 irregular.

346	347
22.4 mm	20.5 mm
1	1

49E, 936

348 - Flan, fields small; rev. outer and inner rims wide. Coin roughly cast. QIAN head lacking. YUAN short. ZHONG head unusually thick. ZHONG tilted to right in addition to BAO. BAO legs asymmetrical, left leg touching outer rim.

349 - Obv. field similar to 348, rev. somewhat larger; obv. outer rim narrow, rev. inner rim not markedly wide. Coin roughly cast. BAO 貝 wider than in 348; legs larger, stubby, asymmetrical, left not reaching outer rim.

350 - Obv. field similar to 340, rev. markedly smaller. QIAN head with nose below middle, angled up; 乙 with long barb. YUAN main bar angled down to right. BAO legs small, left leg touching outer rim.

351 - Fields similar to 340. Coin roughly cast; reverse inner and outer rims low, indistinct. QIAN head straight, long nose in middle, angled up; 日 bar complete; horizontal stroke of 十 above middle. ZHONG head thin. BAO 貝 bars complete, legs nearly symmetrical, left close to outer rim, right not reaching inner rim.

352 - Obv. field somewhat larger than in 340, rev. similar to 340. Characters relatively large. QIAN head with nose below middle, slightly angled up; 日 tapering more on right side than on left; bar thin, complete or nearly so; 乙 with prominent barb. YUAN right leg in rubbed coin unusually thick; typically thinner. ZHONG tall, with moderately thick head; base not reaching outer rim. BAO 王 narrow, 尔 with small dots; 貝 bars nearly complete; legs compact, nearly symmetrical, left leg reaching outer rim, right close to corner of inner rim.

353 - Fields large, as in 327. Outer rims moderately narrow. QIAN, BAO tilted to right. QIAN with small head, horizontal nose in middle; 日 bar incomplete, connecting left. YUAN with right leg deeply curved. ZHONG head large. Head on BAO cap large; 王 narrow, 尔 dots linear; 貝 legs asymmetrical, left thicker than right, reaching outer rim.

354 - Obv. field similar to 340; rev. markedly smaller; rev. inner and outer rims wide. QIAN head straight, nose near base, angled up; horizontal stroke of 十 in middle. YUAN right leg with sharp bend, meeting outer rim close to turn of barb. BAO 王 laterally compressed, irregular; 尔 with small dots; 貝 bars short, centered; legs asymmetrical, thick, neither reaching adjacent rim.

355 - Similar to 354 in most aspects. QIAN head thicker, nose compressed between inner and outer rims; 日 larger; horizontal stroke of 十 above middle. YUAN right leg shorter, less deeply curved. BAO legs thinner; left leg reaching outer rim.

356 - Obv. field as in 340, rev. smaller. QIAN head short; thick nose in middle. ZHONG head thick. BAO 王 narrow but regular; 貝 bars long, nearly complete; legs asymmetrical, left reaching outer rim, right close to corner of inner rim.

357 - Obv. field as in 340, rev. slightly smaller. Obv. outer rim narrow. QIAN head short, nose horizontal, close to middle. ZHONG base short, not connecting to outer rim; 貝 legs asymmetrical; left short and bent, touching outer rim, right longer and straight, not close to inner rim.

358 - Fields as in 357. QIAN head small. YUAN short, with left leg relatively long, deeply curved. Rev. inner rim wide.

359 - Obv. field slightly smaller than in 357, rev. markedly smaller; rev. inner rim wide. QIAN head short, obscured in rubbed coin; 十 irregular. YUAN tall, with short top bar; legs widely spaced. ZHONG 田 not close to outer rim. BAO 貝 with right leg thicker than left, neither touching adjacent rim.

348	349	350	351	352	353
20.0 mm	19.6 mm	20.8 mm	21.7 mm	22.8–23.3 mm	22.5 mm
1	1	1	1	7 · Y276L	1

348 — 585, 349 — 792, 350 — 942, 351 — 1061, 352 — 66-r2, 353 — 589

354	355	356	357	358	359
22.5 mm	22.8 mm	21.6 mm	21.0–21.1 mm	21.0 mm	20.7 mm
1	1	1	2	1	1

354 — 778, 355 — 780, 356 — 784, 357 — 785, 358 — 786, 359 — 787

360 - Fields smaller than in 359. YUAN main bar tilted down to left; right leg evenly curved. ZHONG head thick. BAO 貝 with left leg angular, lower than right, touching outer rim; right straighter, touching corner of inner rim

361 - Fields similar to 360; rev. inner rim narrow. YUAN right leg deeply curved, slightly recurved, with long base. BAO legs similar to 360.

362 - Fields similar to 360; obv. and rev. outer rims moderately wide. QIAN tall, head obscured in rubbed coin. YUAN right leg deeply curved. ZHONG head thick. BAO small; 貝 legs stubby, angled down, left larger than right.

360	361	362
19.6–20.5 mm	19.6 mm	21.7 mm
3	1 · cf. Y289U	1

360 — 794, 361 — 793, 362 — 938

363 - Small flan, fields. Characters obscured in rubbed coin but appear to be irregular. QIAN with wide 日 touching 乙. YUAN short; right leg with sharp bend, long base.

GO BUN SEN (五分銭)

Small coins, 21 mm or less in diameter, with a proportionally large hole. The bar in QIAN 日 is long or short, centered or not, but typically incomplete. YUAN is short and wide, with a long top bar; the hook on the main bar often reaches close to the right leg of BAO, the lower left corner of the inner rim, or both. ZHONG is variable, but 田 is deep, tapering on both sides. BAO is tall, with the head on the cap usually long (368 is an exception); the bars in 貝 are long, and complete or nearly so, and the legs are usually thin and more or less curved. According to Yoshida, the group name he uses is the name used by some Chinese collectors, but the meaning is not entirely clear. The Japanese construction 五分の一 (go bun no ichi) means "one-fifth," so the group name could refer to small, one-fifth value coins. The four varieties Yoshida numbers for this group are all less than 21.1 mm in diameter, but his group seems heterogeneous. Among his four varieties, three show most of the features described above, but Y294 lacks these features and generally appears more similar to the preceding Slanting Yuan group, which also contains a number of coins less than 21 mm in diameter.

364 - QIAN tilted to right; head with long, horizontal nose in middle, 日 with short center bar. YUAN legs long, evenly curved. ZHONG short. BAO with dots in 尔 long, linear; 貝 with bars incomplete, centered; legs long, thin; left leg directed downward; right bent and directed horizontally, each touching adjacent rim.

365 - Fields markedly smaller than in 364; obv. and rev. outer rims moderately wide. QIAN strongly tilted to right; 日 with bar nearly complete, incised from sides. 乙 with strong barb. YUAN short, with hook on main bar nearly reaching right BAO leg. BAO with irregular, incomplete bars; legs thick, right leg longer than left, reaching close to corner of inner rim.

366 - Obv. field slightly larger than in 365, rev. markedly larger; both smaller than in 364. QIAN head unclear in rubbed coin; 日 tilted, bar complete. BAO 貝 with bars shifted right; legs small, left leg truncate, not close to outer rim, right long, thin, reaching corner of inner rim.

367 - Obv. field as in 364, rev. slightly smaller; obv. outer rim narrow. Characters thin. QIAN with left side of 十 horizontal stroke markedly longer than right. ZHONG bar 2 long, extending from inner to outer rim. BAO 貝 with bars long, complete or nearly so; legs thin, similar to those in 364.

368 - Fields slightly smaller than in 365, outer rims wide. Characters small. QIAN 日 with complete bar; with 乙 barb slight; 十 separated from inner rim. YUAN short, with left leg strongly curved, raised or incised from outer rim; barb on right leg slight. BAO 貝 closer to outer than to inner rim; bars complete; legs small, close together, nearly symmetrical, directed horizontally.

363	364	365	366	367	368
18.6 mm	20.6 mm	20.5 mm	20.0 mm	19.2 mm	19.7–20.2 mm
1	1	1	1	1	2
940	788	790	1005	1006	623

GROUPS HAVING TALL YUAN, BLOCKY BAO

YUAN and BAO are in the "clerkly orthodox" calligraphic style

In the last few groups of plain-reverse coins lacking a reverse ring (reverse double rim), YUAN is tall and narrow, with a short top bar; both legs depart the main bar at a steep angle, and the right leg has a tightly curved base. ZHONG is relaxed rather than compact. BAO is blocky, with the cap relatively symmetrical; the 貝 legs, though somewhat variable, are usually thin, often right-angled, and often horizontally directed. In these coins, YUAN and BAO have the stereotyped "clerkly orthodox" calligraphic style seen in Kai Yuan Tong Bao (KYTB; 開元通寶) coins, the main series in the Tang Dynasty, with KAI and TONG replaced by QIAN and ZHONG, as the diagram below illustrates. Groups within KYTB are defined by features of the characters, including TONG, and the names of some of the following QYZB groups in Yoshida's guide reflect similarity to KYTB groups partly defined by TONG. This can be confusing, because QYZB coins obviously have no TONG in the inscription. The Towering Yuan group above (p. 74) has a similarly tall YUAN with a short top bar, but the other characters in that group are different and easily distinguish it from the following groups.

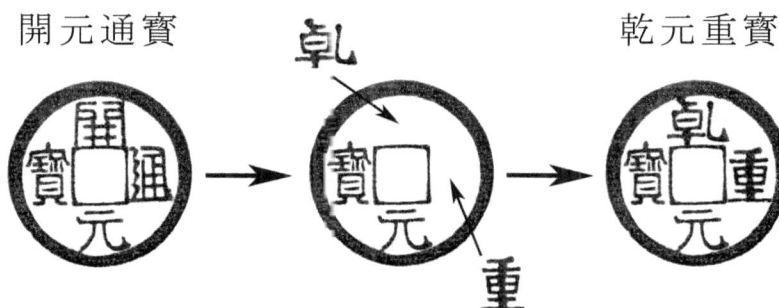

Diagram illustrating the similarity of YUAN and BAO in the QYZB groups below with the "clerkly orthodox" style of the Tang KYTB series (redrawn after Yoshida 2005).

LARGE CHARACTERS, CRAMPED YUAN STYLE
(大字狭元手, *tai ji kô gen zu*)

The name reflects calligraphic similarity to the Large Characters, Cramped Yuan group of 開元通宝. The characters are tall, and large relative to the size of the obverse field. The bar in QIAN 日 is often complete or nearly so, but is short and centered in some varieties. Several groups of varieties show defects in 日 (e.g. see 372–376, 379, 380, 382). ZHONG is close to the inner rim; the head is stubby and degenerate in some varieties, but sometimes the trace remains of a larger, wedge-shaped head lying below the level of relief picked up in a rubbing. BAO 王 is sometimes laterally compressed. Two key features distinguish this group from the following Low Head Tong Style group: 尔 often appears M-shaped due to reduction of the central, vertical stroke, with the long dots on either side fused to the horizontal stroke, and the BAO legs are typically directed diagonally downward, appearing widely spaced. In the Low Head Tong Style group, 尔 is not M-shaped, and the legs are typically somewhat more angular and directed horizontally. Yoshida numbers six varieties in the Large Characters, Cramped Yuan Style group, three with plain reverse.

369 - Characters thin, tilted slightly to right. QIAN tall, with back-curved head incised from outer rim; nose below center, angled up. YUAN, ZHONG, BAO not touching outer rim. ZHONG head thin; base straight. BAO tall; legs symmetrical, curved, thin, reaching slightly below level of inner rim, neither reaching adjacent rim. Very similar to Yoshida's Y302 (flan and field sizes identical), but Y302 has reverse mark.

370 - Obv. field as in 369, rev. field markedly smaller; obv. outer rim narrower, rev. inner rim wider. Flan smaller than in 369. Characters similar, but QIAN head, BAO cap, and ZHONG bar 1 all reaching outer rim.

371 - Fields as in 370; obv. outer rim somewhat narrower. Characters nearly identical to 370, but YUAN right leg touching outer rim, BAO free from outer rim, rev. inner rim appears wider (rubbed coin has slipped reverse). Rubbed coin for 370 is in poor condition due to burial; 370 and 371 could represent same variety.

In next five vars, QIAN 日 has periphery at top and bottom poorly cast and in low relief, with complete center bar and sides prominent and often in higher relief (these features are more evident in coins than in rubbings); 十 also shows high relief.

372 - Outer rims wide. QIAN 日 with left side and center bar in higher relief than rest; 乙 with thick base, swollen barb. YUAN main bar curved, with hook bulbous in one coin, not in other, directed toward corner of inner rim; right leg deeply bent, with long base. BAO 王 with top horizontal stroke separate; right leg of 貝 longer, thicker than left, heavier in one coin than other, just touching corner of inner rim. Rev. inner rim wide. Both coins examined have roseate hole.

373 - Fields as in 372, characters quite similar. Smaller flan, narrower obv. and rev. outer rims. 十 and bar in QIAN 日 in higher relief than rest of 日. YUAN main bar with slightly bulbous hook. Cap of BAO with right shoulder slightly raised; 王 small, laterally compressed, irregular; top of 貝 not connected to sides. BAO legs thin, nearly symmetrical, each just touching adjacent rim. Part of casting sprue evident, indicating that 373 was cast smaller than 372.

374 - Fields similar to 372. Characters tilted slightly to left. QIAN head small, with short horizontal nose. ZHONG head quite small; base of ZHONG angled up. BAO cap with right shoulder slightly raised, as in 373; 王 degenerate, misshapen; 貝 legs large, thick, each touching adjacent rim; right leg larger than

369	**370**	**371**	**372**	**373**	**374**
24.8 mm	23.5 mm	23.5–23.7 mm	23.8–24.0 mm	22.3 mm	22.0 mm
1 cf. Y302	1	2	2	1 Y305L	1 cf. Y305U

left and extending lower than bottom of inner rim. Very similar to Yoshida's Y305U, but QIAN appears to be larger and BAO smaller in 374, with other slight differences.

375 - Fields as in 374, flan larger, outer rims wider. Characters similar but not tilted. Head of ZHONG even smaller than in 374. YUAN with hook on main bar not markedly swollen. BAO 貝 legs similar to 374 but thinner; right leg twice as long as left, neither reaching adjacent rim.

376 - Fields as in 372. Left half of QIAN tilted to right; bar and right side of 日, as well as 十, in high relief. ZHONG head appears reduced, but vestige remains of left half (in low relief, not showing in rubbing) of longer, acute head reaching inner rim. Right leg of BAO 貝 somewhat longer, thicker than left; each leg touching adjacent rim.

In next two vars, QIAN 日 more evenly cast, but 十 in high relief, 日 in low relief

377 - Fields similar to 372. Left half of QIAN tilted to right; base of 乙 drooping toward ZHONG. YUAN right leg with narrow base, reaching outer rim at turn of barb. BAO not touching outer rim; 貝 legs asymmetrical, left leg stubby, not reaching outer rim; right longer, directed toward hook of YUAN.

378 - Obv. field as in 372, rev. field somewhat larger. QIAN 日 with thin outline, complete bar; 乙 with thick, broad base, barb blunt. Hook on main bar of YUAN bulbous; YUAN right leg with barb slight. ZHONG head complete, thin. BAO 貝 with break near top right corner; legs asymmetrical; left thin, reaching outer rim, right thicker, touching corner of inner rim.

375	**376**
24.3 mm	23.3 mm
1	2 Y304

377	**378**
23.3 mm	22.4–22.5 mm
1	2

In following six vars, QIAN 日 has thick outline, with inner field reduced and bar thin, often only faint vestige. In 379, 380, and 382, bar lower than surface of face and/or extremely thin, showing scarcely or not at all in rubbings. These six vars are similar to Yoshida's Y303, which has field sizes similar to 379, but also has reverse mark.

379 - Fields similar to 372; flan smaller, outer rims narrower. Characters nearly identical to those in 372, differing in QIAN 日 having complete, often thick outline, with vestigial bar below level of face, sometimes lacking. BAO 貝 legs asymmetrical, directed diagonally down; left leg thin, reaching outer rim; right leg thicker, longer than left, often somewhat bulbous, touching corner of inner rim.

380 - Fields and characters somewhat larger than in 379. YUAN tall, with left leg above or just reaching outer rim; right leg with narrow base and moderate barb. ZHONG base not reaching outer rim. BAO not touching outer rim; bars in 貝 incomplete, connecting right; legs asymmetrical, similar to those in 379 but neither touching adjacent rim. One coin has weak roseate hole.

381 - Fields as in 380, slightly larger than in 379. Characters nearly identical to 380, but thinner. Differs in having YUAN left leg detached from main bar. BAO 貝 with short bars in center; legs thin, right longer than left. Rubbed coin has weak roseate hole.

382 - Flan and fields smaller than in 379. QIAN 日 with bar scarcely evident; 乙 extending well past right edge of inner rim. YUAN right leg truncated. ZHONG head defective; acute left end of head reaching inner rim but in low relief, not showing in rubbing. Rev. inner rim narrow.

383 - Obv. field as in 379; rev. slightly smaller, rev. inner rim unusually wide. ZHONG head thick; base of ZHONG not reaching outer rim. BAO not touching outer rim; 貝 legs similar in length, angled down, left thicker, not reaching outer rim, right touching corner of inner rim. BAO 王 compressed into indistinct shape; 貝 with break in top; bars short, centered in reduced space with rounded inner corners. Rubbed coin has roseate hole.

384 - Fields similar to 379. QIAN 日 with break at lower right. YUAN raised from outer rim. ZHONG unusual; 田 misshapen, with wings at upper corners and top stroke appearing to form accessory bar (casting defect); base angled strongly upward to right. BAO not touching outer rim; 貝 legs set close to one another, forming inverted V; right leg doubled, extending below bottom of inner rim.

LOW HEAD TONG STYLE (低頭通手, *tei tô tsû zu*)

The name refers to calligraphic similarity to the Low Head Tong group of 開元通宝. QIAN 十 has the left side of the horizontal stroke longer than on the right, and variable (thick or thin; normal, tapering, or turned up). YUAN often has only a slight hook on the main bar. The ZHONG head is long and tapering, distant from the outer rim but reaching the inner rim, or nearly so. The BAO legs are more or less right-angled and directed horizontally. Yoshida numbers 10 varieties, all but one of which have a reverse mark. Several of the coins shown here as having a plain reverse are similar to (and may in fact be) varieties illustrated by Yoshida as having a reverse mark. For example, 387 is probably Yoshida's Y311, which has a faint diagonal bar above the hole on the reverse. In both coins examined here, the mark is so faint as to appear to be a casting irregularity in a plain-reverse coin. Doo (2003: p. 96) illustrates seven coins (24.3–25.8 mm) in this group and lists them as "Valued 10," but does not explain why he considers them as other than value-1.

379	380	381	382	383	384
21.6–23.0 mm	23.3–23.5 mm	23.2 mm	21.1 mm	23.0 mm	23.0 mm
13	2	1	1	1	1

| 234-A | 234-C | 891 | 937 | 890 | 292 |

385 - Outer rims and rev. inner rim moderately wide. QIAN appears to be tilted slightly to left; 日 wide, bar complete; 十 horizontal stroke tapering on right, left end swollen, slightly turned up; 乙 with rounded base and thick barb. ZHONG head reaching inner rim; ZHONG base curving upward to right. BAO separate from outer rim; legs small, asymmetrical, right thicker than left. Above hole on rev. is slight swelling where bar might be expected, not showing in rubbing. Similar to Yoshida's Y308L, but with only vague swelling where reverse mark might be.

386 - Fields similar to 385. Characters thin, larger than in 385; outer rims narrower, QIAN obviously tilted to left, ZHONG head triangular.

387 - Fields somewhat smaller than in 385. QIAN 乙 widely separate from left part of character; shaft straight, tilted to left, with base at right angle to shaft, barb short. Horizontal stroke in QIAN 十 constricted or broken on left side, turned up at end. ZHONG head reaching close to inner rim; 田 narrow, with sides square rather than tapering. BAO separate from outer rim.

388 - Rubbed coin worn, characters thick. Fields similar to 387; outer rims moderately wide. QIAN with left side of horizontal stroke of 十 not constricted; thick, bulbous, turned up at end. Base of QIAN 乙 angled down to right, nearly touching ZHONG head. ZHONG head long, horizontal, meeting upper right corner of inner rim. BAO cap touching outer rim; legs thin, neither leg reaching adjacent rim; larger in worn coin.

385	386
25.1 mm	24.6 mm
1	cf. Y308L	1

| 24 | 865 |

387	388
24.1–24.3 mm	24.4–24.7 mm
2	Y311	2

| 862 | 367A |

389 - Rubbed coin misshapen; fields asymmetrical, similar to 385 or 387, depending on axis measured. QIAN 乙 similar to 388, with base angled down to right, but not as close to ZHONG head; 日 wider, with acute upper-right corner; horizontal stroke of 十 tapering to left. ZHONG head reaching inner rim below upper right corner; 田 rectangular. BAO 王 relatively large, ladderlike; BAO legs nearly symmetrical.

390 - Obv. field as in 387, rev. field slightly smaller. Characters similar to 389. QIAN with horizontal stroke of 十 uniformly narrow, not tapering on left. BAO well separated from outer rim, cap narrower and tilted down to left; 王 narrow; 貝 legs asymmetrical, left much smaller than right. In rubbed coin, hint of possible rev. mark below hole.

391- Field sizes as in 387. QIAN head incised from outer rim; 十 with horizontal stoke meeting 乙; bulb of 乙 separate from outer rim; base at obtuse angle, directed toward ZHONG, with large barb. ZHONG head not reaching inner rim. BAO cap wide, close to outer rim; 貝 legs directed horizontally, left somewhat thicker than right.

392 - Fields as in 387. Crudely cast coin. Characters large, wide, tilted clockwise. QIAN head short; 乙 with large, evenly curved base and unusual, curved barb. ZHONG not touching inner rim; head long; base short, thick, reaching below level of hole rim, not touching inner or outer rims. Head on BAO cap unusually large.

LOW HEAD TONG, LOW YUAN STYLE
(低頭通低元手, *tei tô tsû tei gen zu*)

Again, the name refers to similarity to a particular group of 開元通宝 coins. This QYZB group is similar to the preceding one, but YUAN is shorter, ZHONG 田 tends to be farther from the inner rim, and the ZHONG head is either thinner, shorter, and spaced equidistant from the inner and outer rims, or in some varieties, reduced. The BAO legs are more clearly angular than in the preceding group. Yoshida numbers 18 varieties (excluding those I consider to be in the "Pared Yi" group below), of which four have a plain reverse.

393 - QIAN head back-curved, reaching outer rim, or incised from outer rim in less-worn coins, with horizontal nose in middle; bar in 日 long, complete or slightly incised from one or both sides; 十 connecting with inner rim; 乙 with moderately broad, evenly curved base forming classic hook shape. YUAN right leg evenly curved, reaching outer rim near turn of barb; barb long, angled sharply back. ZHONG head equidistant between inner and outer rims, tapering to point, concave on top. BAO not touching outer rim; cap angled slightly down to left, with narrow head; dots in BAO 尔 long, linear, left dot vertical; bars in 貝 typically long, nearly complete but often incised from one or both sides; 貝 legs nearly symmetrical, directed horizontally, left leg more angular than right. Obv. field occurs in two slightly different sizes but no other features seem to vary consistently with this difference. Most coins have somewhat narrower obv. outer rim than in rubbed coin.

394 - Fields clearly larger than in 393, outer rims narrower; characters thin, slightly larger than in 393. QIAN tall, with small head. BAO 目 with small spine on upper left corner; 貝 left leg larger, lower, more angular than right.

389	390	391	392		393
ca. 25.0 mm	23.5 mm	23.8 mm	23.1 mm		23.2–24.1 mm
1 Y308U?	1	1	1		41 Y316
617	863	493	867		38-r2

394	395	396	397	398	
24.2 mm	23.5–24.5 mm	23.3–24.4 mm	24.6 mm	23.5–23.6 mm	
1	13	9 Y317	1	2	
603	35	29-r4	879	207	

395 - Fields as in 393. QIAN 乙 base more angular, L-shaped than in 393; long bar in 日, centered or shifted left; 十 connecting to inner rim. ZHONG head blunt, rather thick, nearly horizontal. Dots in BAO 尔 long, linear, left dot vertical; 貝 legs thick, nearly symmetrical. Obv. inner rim moderately thick. Break in ZHONG 田 occurred only in rubbed coin.

396 - Fields as in 393. Characters similar to 395, but thinner; QIAN 十 not connecting to inner rim. ZHONG head thinner.

397 - Fields as in 394; larger than in 393. Characters showing same difference from 394 as 395 shows from 393, with base of QIAN 乙 angular rather than evenly curved.

398 - Similar to 395, but obv. field slightly smaller, rev. field markedly smaller; rev. outer rim wide. ZHONG small. BAO cap tilted down to left; 貝 with right leg longer, less angular then left, nearly touching corner of inner rim

WIDE RIMS, PARED YI (潤縁削乙, *katsu en saku otsu*)

Yoshida debated whether these coins should be included in his section with coins having the tall, Kai Yuan-type YUAN, but provisionally placed them in the preceding 'LOW HEAD TONG, LOW YUAN STYLE' group. Yoshida's Y334–339, all but one of which have a plain reverse, form a unified group characterized by wide borders and simplified 乙, and here I list them under a new group name that reflects these features. These coins are often poorly cast, with excess metal tending to fill in spaces within characters, and are often quite worn as well, which complicates identification. QIAN 乙 is obtuse-L shaped, without a barb. The head of ZHONG is reduced, bulbous, and usually bears no vestige of a more extensive head evident in low relief. The right leg of YUAN typically has a strong, back-angled barb.

399 - ZHONG, BAO separate from outer rim. QIAN irregular; 日 small; head tall, with horizontal nose near base. ZHONG tall, narrow; head reduced; right side of bar 1 constricted or detached; base short, curved, not reaching inner or outer rim, left side constricted or detached. BAO 貝 legs small, nearly symmetrical, horizontally directed. Rubbed coin in poor condition and weakly affected by roseate hole.

400 - Fields similar to 399. Characters similar, but QIAN 日, ZHONG 田 larger, shaft of 乙 nearly touching outer rim. QIAN head with short nose just below middle. Left leg BAO twice as thick as right. Rev. inner rim moderately wide.

401 - Obv. field similar to 399, rev. markedly smaller. QIAN head with nose near base. Characters similar to 400, but BAO cap asymmetrical; 貝 legs more symmetrical. Rev. inner and outer rims wider.

402 - Field sizes as in 399. Characters larger than in preceding three vars. Base of ZHONG reaching inner rim. Rev. inner rim narrow.

403 - Rev. field similar to 399, obv. field smaller. QIAN 乙 reaching outer rim; base extending past right edge of inner rim. ZHONG completely free from inner and outer rims; vertical axis of 田 markedly off center; bar 1 short, same length as bar 2; base straight, well above bottom of inner rim.

404 - Fields somewhat asymmetrical, similar to or slightly smaller than in 399. Horizontal stroke in QIAN 十 tilted down to right, right side tapering. QIAN with top of 乙 close to or reaching outer rim; base extending past right edge of inner rim, as in 403. ZHONG inflated, unusual in shape, slight vertical projection at top right of 田 appears to unite 田 with bar 1. ZHONG base long, reaching or nearly reaching outer rim.

405 - Fields asymmetrical in rubbed coin, minimum diameters markedly smaller than in 399; characters small. ZHONG, BAO not touching outer rim; ZHONG not touching inner rim. Outer rims and rev. inner rim wide. QIAN 日 small; head small, with acute nose in middle; 乙 sharp at top, just touching outer rim. QIAN 日 and BAO 目 with short, centered bars. YUAN short; right leg incised from outer rim in less-worn coin, with large barb. ZHONG head longer than in rubbing; tip in low relief; vertical axis of 田 markedly off center. BAO 尓 small, m-shaped, not connected to side of cap; 貝 legs small, angular, horizontally directed, nearly symmetrical. Rubbed coin has weak roseate hole.

STRAIGHT HEAD TONG STYLE (平頭通手, *byô tô tsû zu*)

(Vars 406–409) Variable group. Obv. outer rim not wide. QIAN 日 and ZHONG 田 wide or narrow; base of QIAN 乙 narrow, with or without barb; barb on right leg of YUAN variable; head of ZHONG variable, but usually not as in preceding group. Yoshida lists 21 plain-reverse varieties compared to four here, and interested readers should examine Yoshida's guide. Most of the coins in this group are uncommon to rare.

399	400	401	402	403	404
25.0 mm	24.5 mm	24.5 mm	25.3 mm	24.2 mm	24.1–24.4 mm
1	Y334L	2		1		1		1		5	Y337

587	871	872	873	874	875

406 - Characters thin. QIAN head short, not touching outer rim; base of 乙 narrow, tightly curved, with sharp barb. YUAN right leg not deeply curved. ZHONG short; head diamond shaped, acute tip just touching inner rim; 田 short, wide; ZHONG base straight. BAO legs thin, right longer than left, touching corner of inner rim.

407 - Fields markedly smaller than in 406. QIAN head with long, horizontal nose; 日 wide, nearly rectangular, with bar shifted right; 乙 barb heavy. YUAN right leg sharply bent, with long base and low, blunt barb. ZHONG head large; base slightly above corner of inner rim. BAO tall, narrow; 貝 bars incomplete, centered in circular space; legs asymmetrical, left small, right much longer and reaching inner rim. Rev. inner rim moderately wide. Similar to Y343U, but 407 with smaller obv. field.

408 - Rev. field as in 406, obv. smaller. QIAN with short, straight head, long nose; 日 nearly quadrate, with nearly complete bar; 乙 thick, base narrow, squared. ZHONG tall, head moderately large, equidistant between inner and outer rims; 田 nearly quadrate. BAO narrow, cap reaching outer rim; 王 ladderlike, narrow; 貝 legs moderately thin, left longer than right.

409 - Obv. field as in 406, rev. slightly smaller, obv. outer rim relatively narrow. QIAN head unusually small; 日 nearly square; 乙 sigmoid, not reaching outer rim, barb slight. YUAN tall. ZHONG tall; head small, curved; 田 narrow, swollen; base straight. BAO 貝 with bars long, shifted right; legs thin, angular, directed horizontally, right leg longer than left. Rev. inner rim moderately wide.

405	406	407
24.0–24.1 mm	23.5 mm	22.6 mm
2	cf. Y338	1	Y340	1	cf. Y343

478	864	934

408	409
24.2 mm	23.5 mm
1		1	Y367U

599	881

VALUE-50 STRAY CASTING (当五十彷銖, *tô go jû hô chû*)
(Reverse-ring coins)

Coins in this group have a ring just inside the reverse outer rim, a condition referred to as having a "reverse ring" or "reverse double rim." These are small-sized contemporary imitations of large (diameter about 35 mm), value-50 reverse-ring coins cast officially during the An Shi Rebellion (see the Historical Context section, p. 2). The smaller, usually cruder coins illustrated here were cast by illicit minters who presumably hoped to pass them off as the higher-value coins. Although Doo (2003) refers to these illicit coins as having value 30 to 50, it is doubtful that most of them, particularly those smaller in size than value-1 coins (i.e., less than ca. 25 mm), were valued this high. Whereas many of the varieties of true value-50 coins have a reverse mark, reverse marks are uncommon among the small imitations. Most of the varieties shown here do not appear in Yoshida's catalog, and vice versa, indicating that the small reverse-ring coins are highly diverse and that this diversity remains incompletely documented.

410 - Crudely cast; rubbed coin not very worn, but internal detail of characters not clear; characters thick. QIAN 十 short, with horizontal stroke closer to 日 than to inner rim. QIAN 日 touching 乙; 日 bar complete; shaft of 乙 thick, uniform in width, with slight bulb, meeting outer rim; base angled down toward ZHONG. Right leg of YUAN deeply curved, broadly meeting outer rim. ZHONG with large head meeting inner rim; bar 1 incised from outer rim; base separate from outer rim. BAO legs thick, asymmetrical, left larger than right. Reverse ring irregular in width. Similar to Yoshida's Y108U, but all three coins examined here have 日 touching 乙 and hole impinging on 十 to a greater extent.

411 - Obv. field as in 410, rev. somewhat smaller; obv. and rev. outer rims narrower. Similar to Yoshida's Y108L, but QIAN 日 impinging on 乙, overlapping it for about 2/3 width of shaft; right leg of YUAN less deeply curved.

412 - Obv. field asymmetrical; largest obv. diameter and rev. similar to 410. Rubbed coin has slipped reverse. Characters slightly smaller than in 410/411, slightly tilted to left; ZHONG base reaching outer rim. Obverse side of rubbed coin shows raised line as result of crack in casting mold running diagonally across upper right corner of hole, indicating coin was not face-ground or worn after casting. Characters crudely cast, with internal detail obscured.

413 - Fields somewhat smaller than in 410. Characters similar to preceding three entries, but outer rim carved away from around QIAN head; ZHONG bar 1 reaching outer rim.

414 - Fields similar to 410. Characters similar, but better cast. QIAN head smaller; 日 narrower, well separated from 乙, inside space reduced, with rounded inside corners, bar nearly complete, incised from sides; 乙 with conspicuous bulb, not meeting outer rim. ZHONG bar 1 and base reaching outer rim. BAO with left side of cap appressed to outer rim; 貝 bars long, connecting left; legs thin, asymmetrical, left thicker than right, neither quite reaching adjacent rim.

415 - Fields as in 410. Characters thinner, better cast. QIAN with bar in 日 long, incomplete, shifted right; 乙 shaft with weak bulb, incised from outer rim. YUAN, ZHONG, and BAO incised from outer rim. ZHONG with relatively thin head. BAO 尔 with right dot exaggerated, teardrop-shaped, left dot linear, vertical, middle stroke thin; bars in BAO 貝 long, centered; legs small, angular, symmetrical, horizontally directed, each nearly reaching adjacent rim. Rev. ring thick, scarcely separate from outer rim.

410	411	412	413	414	415
25.8–26.2 mm	25.1 mm	25.3 mm	25.2 mm	25.5 mm	26.1 mm
3	cf. Y108U	1	cf. Y108L	1		1		1		1	

947   946   956   153   957   958

416 - Obv. field as in 410, rev. slightly larger. Characters similar to 410, but larger. YUAN right leg with sharper, more angular bend. ZHONG bar 1 and base reaching outer rim. Rev. ring thin, field inside ring somewhat larger than in 410. Coin only partly edge-filed; characters in low relief with poor detail, faces of coin granular, not finished.

417 - Fields similar to 416; characters smaller, better cast, with some internal detail. QIAN head with nose at base, angled up. YUAN right leg reaching outer rim near turn of barb; barb small; left leg truncate (casting defect?). ZHONG bar 1 not reaching outer rim; base incised from rim. BAO legs nearly symmetrical, left leg reaching outer rim, right not reaching inner rim. Rev. ring thin, as in 416.

418 - Fields and characters smaller than in 410. QIAN head tall, with short nose in middle, slightly angled up; 日 with sharp projection from upper left corner; 日 bar incomplete, centered; shaft of 乙 straight, with slight bulb, reaching outer rim. ZHONG head triangular; bar 1 not reaching and bar 2 reaching outer rim; base straight, reaching outer rim. Head on BAO cap large, triangular; 目 markedly trapezoidal, right side taller than left; bars thin, complete; 貝 legs long, slightly turned up, right leg thicker than left, each reaching adjacent rim.

419 - Fields and characters similar to 418; QIAN head larger, with longer nose; 乙 shaft curved; YUAN main bar tilted down to right; right leg with back-turned barb. Rev. inner rim moderately wide. Reverse ring thick, scarcely distinct from outer rim in rubbed coin.

416	417
26.1 mm	26.4 mm
1	1

950   951

418	419
24.5 mm	24.8 mm
1	1

961   36

420 - Fields similar to 418. Characters similar to 418, but poorly cast, with little internal detail. QIAN head shorter; 乙 with heavy, wide barb. ZHONG base curved upward from corner of inner rim. BAO tilted slightly to left; cap with small head; 貝 legs thick, bulbous, nearly symmetrical. Reverse ring thick, scarcely separated from outer rim; no separation showing in rubbing.

421 - Fields similar to 418. QIAN 乙 well separated from 日; conspicuous bulb on shaft. YUAN right leg with sharp bend. ZHONG head rounded rather than triangular; head on BAO cap rounded rather than triangular. Rev. ring thick.

422 - Obv. field clearly smaller than in 418, rev. slightly smaller; obv. outer rim moderately wide. Characters smaller than in preceding vars. QIAN head with short nose arising near base, angled up; dot or excess metal between nose of QIAN head and bulb of shaft. YUAN left leg only slightly curved. ZHONG short; bar 1 incised from outer rim; base reaching outer rim. BAO legs asymmetrical, right larger than left, reaching below bottom of inner rim.

423 - Obv. field as in 422, rev. field markedly smaller. Characters small. QIAN head small, thick, with weak nose near middle, angled up; 日 with complete bar in rounded space. YUAN right leg taller than in 422. ZHONG 田 strongly tapering on right; upper corners of 田 acute. BAO cap appressed to outer rim, head on cap tall; 貝 legs asymmetrical, left thick, right tapering and acute, each reaching adjacent rim.

Next three vars have base of 乙 wide, extending well past right edge of inner rim.

424 - Large flan, fields. QIAN tall, with tall head having nose near base, angled up. ZHONG head thin. Rev. ring thin, distinct from outer rim. Similar to Yoshida's Y112, in which flan and obv. field are markedly larger, reverse field slightly larger; in Y112, bottom part of QIAN 十 missing. Rubbed coin with large casting gap in lower left quadrant (obv. view).

425 - Flan size and obv. field similar to 410 above; rev. field markedly larger than in 410, rev. outer rim thin. Characters tilted slightly to left. QIAN head short, with nose near base, angled up; bar in 日 complete, tilted; 十 with horizontal stroke detached on right; 乙 with thick bulb tapering down top half of shaft. YUAN thick, squat. ZHONG base thick, strongly angled up to right, reaching outer rim. BAO cap with right shoulder slightly raised; 貝 bars thin, complete in reduced space; 貝 legs large, left larger and lower than right, each reaching adjacent rim. Rev. inner rim wide. Ring thin, well separated from thin outer rim. Similar to Yoshida's Y113U (which also has horizontal stroke of 十 detached), but Y113U has smaller rev. field and wider rev. outer rim, and characters not tilted.

426 - Obv. field somewhat smaller than in 425, rev. markedly smaller, obv. outer rim narrow. Characters very similar, but all tilting strongly to left. QIAN 十 with horizontal stroke detached on right, as in 425, but reaching 乙. YUAN right leg thick, aberrant. BAO left leg unusually thick, angled downward.

427 - Fields smaller than in 410; similar to 418. Characters except YUAN small. QIAN head with nose near base, angled up; 日 narrow, with incomplete bar centered in rounded space; 乙 with distinct bulb, incised from outer rim. YUAN with short top bar. ZHONG head moderate in size, triangular; 田 short and wide, not close to inner rim, strongly tapering on right side. ZHONG bar 1 and base reaching inner and outer rims. Bars in BAO 貝 nearly complete, shifted left; BAO legs thin, right leg not reaching inner rim.

428 - Fields similar to 427. QIAN 日 with complete bar; 乙 lacking bulb, reaching outer rim. ZHONG head long, thin; 田 deep; bar 1 and base not quite reaching outer rim. Bars in BAO 貝 thin, complete, in reduced space; 貝 legs thick, angular, nearly symmetrical, each reaching adjacent rim.

420	421	422	423	424	425
25.1 mm	24.5 mm	25.2 mm	23.8 mm	28.2 mm	26.7 mm
1	1	1	1	1	1	cf. Y113U

1056 · 962 · 963 · 955 · 948 · 972

426	427	428	429	430	
ca. 25.0 mm.	24.8 mm	25.0 mm	24.8–25.5 mm	25.0 mm	
1	1	1	6	1	

1055 · 959 · 954 · 952 · 960

429 - Fields similar to 427. QIAN head incised from outer rim in unworn coins; nose slightly below middle, slightly angled up; 日 with long center bar in space with rounded inside corners; 乙 with conspicuous circular bulb, not reaching outer rim. YUAN right leg meeting outer rim at turn of barb. ZHONG 田 touching inner rim, taller on right than on left; upper right corner extended; ZHONG base short, angled up, distant from outer rim. BAO cap tilted down to left; 貝 with long bars, nearly complete, incised from sides; legs not angular, nearly symmetrical, each just touching adjacent rim. Five of six coins are poorly cast and worn; rubbed coin fairly well cast on obv. side, poorly cast on rev.

430 - Fields similar to 427. Characters tilted slightly to left. YUAN tall. QIAN impinged by hole; head thin, nose near base, angled up. YUAN right leg touching outer rim at turn of barb. ZHONG with thin, triangular head, nearly reaching inner rim; bar 1 not reaching outer rim, base reaching outer rim. BAO cap symmetrical. Coin relatively well cast; rev. ring and outer rim crisp, in high relief. Outer edge only partly finished; mostly rough with excess metal. Outer rim in upper right quadrant (obv. view) of rubbed coin missing due to incomplete casting.

431 - Obv. field somewhat smaller than in 430, rev. somewhat smaller; rev. field inside ring quite small. QIAN head nearly straight, nose slightly below middle, horizontal; 日 scarcely tapering; 乙 shaft thickened toward top, just touching outer rim, barb lacking. Hole impinging on YUAN top bar and ZHONG. ZHONG head large, irregular; 田 markedly tapering on right; bar 1 and base reaching inner and outer rims. BAO 貝 bars complete, in reduced space; legs thick, asymmetrical, left angular, reaching outer rim, right bulbous, incised from inner rim. Obv. outer rim narrower in rubbing than it actually is because edge tapering toward obverse side. Reverse ring thick, nearly completely fused with outer rim.

432 - Obv. field as in 427, rev. somewhat larger. Rev. inner rim narrow. Obverse side unusually well cast compared to most other reverse-ring coins of this size. QIAN and YUAN tall. QIAN head unusually tall, nearly straight, nose slightly below middle, slightly angled up; 日 scarcely tapering, bar incomplete, shifted left; 乙 sigmoid, with small, curved bulb, well separate from outer rim. YUAN with top bar short; right leg raised. ZHONG with tiny head; 田 nearly touching inner rim; base straight, just touching outer rim. BAO legs small, asymmetrical, right longer than left, neither reaching adjacent rim. Reverse ring thin.

433 - Rev. field similar to 432, obv. somewhat larger. Characters larger than in 432; hole large; obv. inner rim slight. QIAN and YUAN tall. QIAN tilted slightly to left; head tall, nearly straight as in 432, with thin, horizontal nose; 日 bar incomplete, centered; 乙 shaft thickened at upper end, distant from outer rim, base angled down, barb small. ZHONG relaxed, head irregular; base sraight, just touching outer rim; left dot in 尔 thin, linear, right dot teardrop-shaped; bars in 貝 thin, complete; legs horizontal.

434 - Maub fields and rev. field inside ring slightly smaller than in 431, rev. inner rim close to outer rim. QIAN head erect, horizontal nose near base; bar in 日 short, incomplete, shifted right in reduced space; 乙 shaft with small, circular bulb, not reaching outer rim. YUAN short, right leg with narrow, tightly curved base and prominent barb. ZHONG head long, reaching inner rim; ZHONG base curved up to right, reaching outer rim. Reverse ring nearly completely fused with outer rim, with only faint traces indicating its presence, not evident in rubbing.

435 - Obv. field similar to 434; rev. field markedly larger. Obv. outer rim wide. QIAN head short, with nose (obscured in rubbed coin) sandwiched between 日 and outer rim. ZHONG head large, reaching inner rim; bar 1 and base reaching outer rim. YUAN unusually short, with left leg long and recurved, as in Prancing Yuan group. BAO tall; legs thick, asymmetrical, right much larger than left. Rev. ring thin, close to outer rim. Coin appears to be poorly cast, with little detail in characters, rather than appreciably worn.

Remaining reverse-ring entries are crudely cast coins with internal details of characters often obscured; most vars less than 24 mm in diameter, and many less than 23 mm. Obv. inner rim usually quite thin, often lacking around much of hole; hole often infringing on one or more characters, one or more of which may be tilted relative to hole. QIAN 日 has short or long incomplete bar, often in rounded or oblong space (long, incomplete bar can appear complete in worn coins); 乙 usually with thick barb. ZHONG 田 closely appressed to inner rim; in most vars, ZHONG with short base, not reaching outer rim. It is unclear what aspects of design or casting process caused some or all characters to be tilted and hole to infringe on them.

436 - Characters large, except for ZHONG; ZHONG, YUAN slightly tilted to right. QIAN tall, with short, thick head, nose near base; 日 with long bar appearing complete in worn coin; 乙 shaft with enlarged bulb. ZHONG short, impinged by hole. BAO legs thick; left leg obscured in rubbed coin. BAO cap nearly symmetrical, with semicircular head.

431	432	433	434	435	436
25.0 mm	25.7 mm	25.5 mm	24.3 mm	26.1 mm	24.8 mm
1	1 · Y120	1	1	1	1

476	944	269	270	1093	1094

437 - Obv. field markedly smaller than in 436, rev. somewhat smaller. Obv. inner rim slight. Characters small, tilted to right. QIAN head with horizontal nose near middle; left end of 十 horizontal stroke swollen; 日 thickened on top and left side, with bar short, centered in reduced space with rounded inside corners; center of bar in low relief, with ends appearing as dots in rubbing. 乙 shaft with long bulb, reaching outer rim; barb tall, blunt. YUAN main bar with hook end thickened. ZHONG head moderately large, nearly reaching inner rim; 田 scarcely tapering. Vertical stroke between BAO dots detached from horizontal, giving three dots; 貝 bars appear to be complete; legs thick, asymmetrical, right shorter and thicker than left, each meeting adjacent rim.

438 - Fields similar to 437; obv. outer rim narrower. Very similar to 437, but coin cast smaller, as evidenced by casting sprue. Characters similar. QIAN 乙 shaft with expanded bulb. YUAN main bar with only slight hook; left leg longer than in 437, straight toward end.

439 - Obv. field somewhat larger than in 437, rev. similar. Hole large; slight obv. inner rim discernable only to right of BAO; absent around rest of hole. Characters tilted slightly to left. QIAN 乙 with wide, angular, L-shaped base. YUAN legs close together; right leg not vertical. BAO 貝 legs similar to 437.

440 - Fields similar to 437. All characters tilted strongly to right; QIAN, YUAN impinged by hole. QIAN with bar in 日 long, incomplete, in reduced space; bulb of 乙 distinct. ZHONG 田 tapering on both sides. Hook on main bar of YUAN slight, nearly touching left corner of inner rim. Rubbed coin worn; rev. ring scarcely separate from outer rim.

437	438
23.8–24.3 mm	22.8–23.2 mm
4	2

945	966

439	440
23.9 mm	23.5–24.0 mm
1	2

1026	989

441 - Fields similar to 437. Characters similar to 440, all slightly tilted to right, though less than in 440; characters more robust. QIAN head shorter; 日 with bar complete or nearly so in oval space; 乙 shaft uniformly thick, with larger barb. YUAN right leg with sharp bend, shape inside base and barb quadrate. Hook of YUAN touching corner of inner rim and nearly touching right leg of BAO. Left leg of BAO thicker than right; right leg angled down, end acute, reaching corner of inner rim.

442 - Obv. field smaller than in 437, rev. slightly smaller. Very similar to 441, but cast smaller, as evidenced by casting sprue; characters smaller. Only YUAN strongly tilted; BAO slightly tilted. Head of BAO cap relatively small. BAO 貝 legs small, thin; right leg angled down, acute, converging with hook of YUAN at corner of inner rim.

443 - Fields smaller than in 437. Coin not appreciably worn, but characters in low relief, lacking detail. Characters all tilted to right and all partly infringed by hole. Bar in QIAN 日 long, incomplete in reduced space. Hook of YUAN touching corner of inner rim. Base of ZHONG thick. BAO positioned high, cap nearly touching horizontal stroke 十; right leg of 貝 above corner of hole. BAO legs thick, asymmetrical, right leg lower than left. Reverse ring thick.

444 - Fields similar to 437. YUAN strongly tilted to right. Rev. inner rim narrow. QIAN head with nose near bottom, horizontal. YUAN left leg long, shallowly curved. ZHONG head thin, triangular, acute, just reaching inner rim; bar 1 not perpendicular to inner rim; left side bar 2 appears to be short, truncate; base thick. Head of BAO cap truncate, forming low swelling, with or without sharp projection. Left leg of BAO 貝 thin, angled down, close to outer rim; right leg thick, blunt, reaching close to corner of inner rim, not close to hook of YUAN. To left of YUAN, sharp projection arising from outer rim; two coins of var. 444 and one coin representing var. 445 have similar projection in same place. Reverse ring thinner in example of 444 not shown in rubbing.

445 - Obv. field smaller than in 444, rev. as in 444. Characters except BAO smaller than in 444. QIAN head small, with thin nose in middle. YUAN left leg short, raised. ZHONG head thick; ZHONG base short, swollen at each end. Head on BAO cap truncate, leaving sharp projection, as in 444; 貝 legs moderately thin, splayed, nearly symmetrical, each reaching adjacent rim. Reverse ring moderately thin. To left of YUAN, small projection from outer rim.

446 - Fields similar to 442. Characters similar to 441–443. Rev. field markedly smaller than in 441, characters smaller than in 441, larger than in 442; characters tilted slightly to right. QIAN head with nose below middle, angled up. ZHONG head thick, blunt; ZHONG base quite thick. BAO cap sloping down to left; 貝 legs thick, blunt (thinner in one coin), right leg close to corner of inner rim.

447 - Obv. field slightly smaller than in 442, rev. field somewhat larger. Rev. inner rim narrow. Characters similar to 446, but QIAN head small, with short, horizontal nose near base; part of outer rim trimmed away to expose QIAN head; ZHONG head thick, tapering, merging with inner rim; BAO cap narrower, not sloping down to left.

448 - Fields similar to 447. Characters small, especially ZHONG; all characters tilted to right, infringed by hole. QIAN head small, with nose in middle, horizontal. ZHONG head small, reaching inner rim. BAO cap with small head; 貝 legs large, bulbous.

449 - Similar to 446, but coin oblong, taller than broad; hole taller than broad. Maximum obv. and minimum rev. field diameters similar to 446. Characters slightly tilted to right. QIAN head short; obscured but appears to have horizontal nose in middle.

441	442	443	444	445	446
23.8–24.3 mm	22.9 mm	22.4 mm	23.1–23.3 mm	22.7 mm	22.5–23.3 mm
3	1	1	2	1	4
969	967	990	23	981	982

447	448	449	450	451	
22.8 mm	22.8 mm	22.3 x 23.3 mm	22.5 mm	22.4 mm	
1	1	1	1	1	
983	979	61	970	977	

450 - Obv. field similar to 437, rev. somewhat smaller; obv. outer rim moderately narrow. Hole broader than tall. QIAN, BAO infringed by hole. YUAN main bar tilted down to right. Bar in QIAN 日 long, centered. Nose of QIAN head below middle, horizontal. QIAN 乙 appears tilted, but this is casting error involving excess metal over shaft; shaft of 乙 actually perpendicular to hole and just touching outer rim; base L-shaped. ZHONG compact, with large head; base wide, reaching outer rim. BAO 尔 with vertical stroke between dots detached, appearing as third dot; 貝 left leg not reaching outer rim; right leg obscured. Reverse ring thin, distinct. Obverse crudely cast, with excess metal in several places, but with detail in characters.

451 - Fields somewhat smaller than in 450; characters similar but not tilted; BAO and to some extent QIAN and YUAN infringed by hole. ZHONG, BAO lacking internal detail. QIAN head thick, with nose at base, angled up; base of 乙 narrow, with long barb. YUAN thick. ZHONG with smaller head than in 450. BAO short, with left leg large, blunt, reaching outer rim; right leg small, touching corner of inner rim. Reverse ring thicker, less distinct.

452 - Small flan; substantial, 1.0 mm thick; poorly cast. As in Yoshida's Y111, rubbed coin has gap in vicinity of left side of BAO cap and distinctive gap in left side of ZHONG 田.

453 - Larger flan than 452; fields somewhat larger. Characters similar, but larger. Similar to 452 in having gap in vicinity of left side of BAO cap and another in left side of ZHONG 田, as seen in 452. BAO right leg displaced, shifted away from corner of hole.

Addenda: additional varieties recognized and added after the catalog was compiled.

454 - Wide Characters group. Flan size similar to 174 but obv. field slightly larger, rev. markedly larger than in 174; obv. outer rim narrow. QIAN with thin nose above middle, horizontal; 日 bar long, shifted right. YUAN left leg raised from rim; right leg with sharp bend, meeting rim at turn of barb. ZHONG head small, thin. BAO 貝 with bars irregular; bottom bar complete, top bar short and centered; 王 tall, tilted; dots in 尔 thin, linear, angled outward. BAO legs angular, asymmetrical, left smaller than right (incompletely cast?), neither meeting adjacent rim.

455 - Prancing Yuan group; similar to 198, but having thick ZHONG head and left dot in BAO 尔 vertical rather than angled out. BAO 王 in rubbed coin has lower two horizontal strokes broken on right side, becoming dots; other coin has only middle stroke as dot on right.

456 - Slanting Yuan group; should follow entry 357. Fields and characters similar to 357, but QIAN, ZHONG, BAO tilted to right, YUAN main bar tilted down to left. QIAN 乙 with wider, angular base. YUAN main bar with hook more pronounced. ZHONG head thin; bar 1 not perpendicular to inner rim. BAO 貝 with right leg pointing toward hook of YUAN, as in 357, but right leg thicker than left.

457 - Towering Yuan group. Fields slightly larger than in 265, characters thin. This coin was used in wear example (p. 19). Quite similar to Yoshida's Y232U, although rev. field in latter somewhat smaller. Abundance and status unclear. Few coins in this group have characters (especially head of QIAN) this thin, but as wear example shows, QIAN head can become markedly thicker and larger with surface finishing and/or wear, resembling other putative varieties in Towering Yuan group.

452	453	454	455	456	457
20.3 mm	21.0 mm	23.0 mm	25.0 mm	19.7 mm	22.3 mm
1	Y111	1		1		2		1		1	cf. Y232U

| 949 | 965 | 842 | 828 | 939 | 3-wear 0 |

Appendix 1. Cleaning cash coins

The sabi, or age coating of salts and minerals, gives ancient coins an attractive ancient appearance, but it can also severely obscure characters necessary for identification to variety, and furthermore prohibit clear rubbings. Thus I cleaned most of the QYZB coins I examined. While some purists choose never to clean cash coins, it is noteworthy that most museums routinely clean heavily encrusted, ancient to medieval Asian and Western bronze coins, for the simple reason that encrusted coins are often not amenable to study. I must note, however, that most collectors prefer that their ancient coins look ancient, and cleaning can reduce the sale value of cash coins.

When I first started cleaning antique bronze coins, I used dilute HCl (hydrochloric acid, also called muriatic acid). This is absolutely the worst thing possible, as it leads to a chemical reaction with copper that produces cuprous chloride (CuCl). CuCl on coins reacts with moisture in the air to produce more HCl, which in turn produces more CuCl. This reaction becomes self-sustaining, leading to what is called "bronze disease," evident as soft, powdery, light-green patches on coins (not to be confused with hard, green malachite). With time, bronze disease eats deep pits into coins, effectively destroying them.

Fortunately, bronze disease is treatable; information is available on the Internet, and also see Scott (2002). I have found that products used to remove chlorine from tap water before filling freshwater fish aquaria produce by far the best results in curing bronze disease; these are non-toxic and effective in highly diluted form. The product I use is ContraChlorine™ made by Tetra Company. Various similar products are sold in pet stores worldwide, although I don't know their relative effectiveness. To treat coins, I brush them with a brass-bristle brush to remove the powdery green CuCl and then soak them overnight in a solution containing a few drops of ContraChlorine™ in 50–100 mL of water. After the soak, I rinse them well in deionized water and finally rub them dry with a cloth. A ContraChlorine™ solution can also be used to tone bronze and copper coins that have become too bright through cleaning; an overnight soak will leave them with a more attractive, antique-brownish pseudo-patina.

For cleaning I now use only the white vinegar one buys in grocery stores. Vinegar contains acetic acid (CH_3COOH), which lacks chloride ions. A citric acid solution will also work, and some people claim it is even better. These organic acids clean much more slowly than HCl but minimize eventual problems with bronze disease. For cleaning, I place coins in vinegar overnight and then brush them with a brush having fine brass bristles. It is critical not to use a steel-bristle brush, as this will scratch bronze coins. Brass-bristle brushes can usually be found in hardware or automotive-supply stores, because mechanics use them for cleaning engines.

For lightly encrusted coins, an overnight soak and single brushing will often remove all of the encrusting malachite, a hard, green carbonate of copper. Thick patches of malachite will require continued soaking and brushing, as necessary. QYZB coins can be left for several days to a week in vinegar without adverse effects, although it is probably best to leave them in only as long as necessary. When the coins are sufficiently clean, I rinse them several times and then soak them overnight in deionized water to remove all of the acetic acid. Deionized water is preferable to tap water because the latter often contains appreciable amounts of chlorine. Surprisingly, the sabi on most Asian cash coins contains a lot of just plain dirt; brushing 50 or so encrusted coins after soaking them in vinegar will leave an astonishing amount of fine silt in the sink. Depending on the source, a high proportion of the previously buried coins in some bulk lots are simply dirty and can be sufficiently cleaned by soaking in water and brushing, without any other treatment.

Malachite itself is so hard it can damage even a steel tool and must be removed by acid treatment. However, neither HCl nor vinegar will remove certain reddish, brownish, or whitish minerals that occur in thin layers along with the malachite. If these minerals remain after vinegar treatment and obscure features necessary for identification, they must be removed mechanically with a sharp, hardened-steel tool. It is easy to gouge or scratch coins in this way, but with practice and a steady hand, mechanical cleaning can be accomplished with minimal damage.

Not all Asian cash coins are equally amenable to cleaning. Even vinegar will completely strip brass coins or those with high copper content, such as many coins from the Qing Dynasty, leaving them in an unattractive bright state. Acid treatments will also adversely affect zinc coins, lead coins, and bronze coins with a high lead content, because even weak acids will dissolve zinc or lead, and the removal of encrusting minerals may expose characters already partly damaged by the formation of the minerals. Fortunately, most QYZB are quite amenable to cleaning. The bronze in these coins is relatively durable, and the characters are largely undamaged under mineral encrustations. Vinegar rarely reduces QYZB coins to a bright state, but leaves them with a pleasing antique-brown color. Although QYZB with an unusually high copper content will become bright upon cleaning, such coins are rarely encountered, and the fact that they have high copper content is in itself useful information.

Appendix 2. Purchasing cash coins

Sellers on Ebay and Yahoo Auction Japan frequently offer individual Asian cash coins from among the thousands of common varieties for up to US$10 or more per coin, banking on the buyers' misconception that ancient and medieval coins are generally uncommon or rare. Even worse, some unscrupulous Internet sellers offer common Asian cash under the "buy now" option for hundreds of dollars apiece. I recently saw a Tang Dynasty Huichang Kai Yuan coin for sale for $450 (worth at most $5), and common Northern Song varieties for roughly $100 apiece (worth less than $1 apiece). Unsuspecting buyers might be fooled into believing that these coins are rare, thinking that no one would have the audacity to engage in such egregious scams in public view. Although obviously there are ethical issues, technically these sellers are not doing anything illegal if they do not advertise the coins as rare, but let the high prices imply that they are.

Many Asian cash coin types were manufactured by the millions and are common. Even now (2020), QYZB can occasionally be found on Ebay in non-cleaned bulk lots for roughly 70 cents US per coin. Other types of cash coins, each of which has enough common varieties to occupy a collector for years, can be bought even more cheaply. Bulk lots of some Chinese Han Dynasty (206 BC–25 AD) types can still be found on the Internet for 50–60 cents per coin. Chinese Tang Dynasty Kai Yuan Tong Bao (開元通宝), Northern Song Dynasty (many reign titles), and Japanese Kan'ei Tsûhô (寛永通宝), with each type having hundreds of varieties, can still be found in bulk lots for as little as 30–40 cents each (Kan'ei Tsûhô, sometimes as little as 15 cents each on Yahoo Auction Japan). Several years ago, Chinese Qing Dynasty (1644–1912) coins were perhaps the cheapest type at 15–20 cents each, but bulk prices for these coins have increased steadily to $US 0.50–1.00 per coin, presumably due to economic prosperity in China leading to an increased number of collectors there. A few years ago, Vietnamese cash coins, of which there are many reign titles and varieties, could be found for 30–80 cents each, depending on the type, or 13–15 cents each for the diminutive coins collectively called "small cash." While the small cash are still inexpensive, prices of other types seem to be steadily increasing and diverse bulk lots increasingly difficult to find.

Of course, prices for any coins purchased individually will be higher than the quantity or "wholesale" prices achieved through purchasing bulk lots. As prices increase overall, dealers might tend to increasingly sell coins individually. However, it takes greater effort to sell individual coins, and dealers will reach a point of diminishing returns due to variety collectors' unwillingness to pay relatively high prices for single examples of common varieties. Thus I expect that an equilibrium will be reached whereby bulk lots are still available but at somewhat higher prices than previously.

In all countries that produced cash coins, some dynasties, reigns, or eras produced fewer coins and these are more expensive now on average, but usually not exorbitantly so; cash coins from the Ming Dynasty, Southern Song Dynasty, and Korea fall into this category. On the other hand, production was unusually low in some eras, such as the Chinese Yuan Dynasty, and these coins are justifiably pricey. And of course, genuinely uncommon or rare cash varieties are scattered across all relevant countries' dynasties, reigns, and eras.

Most current collectors will already be aware of these cautions about Internet purchasing, which are aimed at interested people just beginning to collect Asian cash coins. Buyers incapable of assessing the authenticity and value of coins or the integrity of dealers are well advised to steer clear of expensive coins. Again, "buy the book before you buy the coin." For anything over a few dollars, know what you are buying, whether it is genuine, and how much it is actually worth.

It is also important when purchasing coins from the Internet to know the relevant import regulations in the destination country to which the coins will be shipped. These regulations vary greatly from country to country. For example, Japan permits the importation of collectible antiques, including antique coins, with no restrictions and with no import duty, although a "luxury tax" can be charged on purchases from some numismatic auction houses in Europe that are requried to ship with an export permit, somehow triggering the luxury tax. To my knowledge, the USA likewise does not bar the import of numismatic items and there is no duty on them. In other cases, while countries do not restrict the import of coins, they charge an import duty on any shipments above a certain threshold value.

At the other end of the spectrum are countries that actively discourage transactions involving certain categories of ancient and antique coins. Italy, Greece, and Turkey, for example, with extensive material histories, have enacted strict laws to try to preserve their archaeological heritage, and each country considers ancient (and in some cases medieval) numismatic items produced in that country to belong to the government, as part of the national heritage. Customs inspectors in these countries are remarkably diligent, and various ancient or antique coins they detect entering or exiting their country are subject to confiscation. In short, whatever country buyers are in, they should become familiar with that country's laws regarding the import of coins before making Internet purchases.

www.ingramcontent.com/pod-product-compliance
Lightning Source LLC
LaVergne TN
LVHW081317060426
835509LV00015B/1564